BETTER
BELIEVE

A STORY OF HOPE

RUBY LEE TUESDAY

Order this book online at www.trafford.com
or email orders@trafford.com

Most Trafford titles are also available at major online book retailers.

Printed in the United States of America.

ISBN: 978-1-4907-4992-1 (sc)
ISBN: 978-1-4907-4994-5 (hc)
ISBN: 978-1-4907-4993-8 (e)

Library of Congress Control Number: 2014919435

Trafford rev. 12/29/2014

 www.trafford.com

North America & international
toll-free: 1 888 232 4444 (USA & Canada)
fax: 812 355 4082

CONTENTS

DEAR READER

Dear reader, I write to you because I would like to share my story with you. It is a story of determination, losing track, passion, betrayal, friendship, and most of all, it is a tale of hope that might help you get along better with your life or see things in a new perspective than you would before reading this book. You can achieve whatever you want in life if you only believe it. I have been looking for happiness all my life, and in order to find it, I had to start listening to my conscience and start doing the right things. Not only was it the right thing to do to others, but it also took away the bad emotions connected to not doing right and lit up the way for joy to come into my life. I just learned that all things that are keeping you doing things you don't like are sin. We may call them "addiction this" and "addiction that," but they are all sin. I would have resented hearing that at the top of my addiction, but I know now that the enemy, the devil, is the one who keeps this knowledge away from your heart. The devil does not want you to be happy, and what I found after talking to a huge number of people is that everybody just wants to be happy. So I ask, Dear God, Father in heaven, please help me write my story as honest and helpful as I can. Help it help this reader find what he or she is looking for in their lives and, most of all, find the love for themselves and be their own best friend and treat others in the same way. Be who you are, but be your best version of you. And help me try and be the best version of me. This I ask in your son Jesus Christ's name. Amen.

A SUMMARY OF THE
MEMORIES OF A PAST

It was a summer day in 1979 that this baby child was born. She resisted and twisted for two weeks, and when she finally came, her forehead came first. She was nearly strangled by the cord around her neck. The doctors took her and ran out of the room. She never connected with her mother, and her mother never connected with her. Her surroundings were wild. She had a sister and, later on, got a brother. They were all raised in different parts of the house, isolated from one another. The house was haunted, and her room reminded of a prison cell. Besides a tiny window in the roof, there was no light coming into her darkness. Outside her window was the dark and starlit sky. She cried at night, wondering why—why she had to live above the deadly living room. Voices and hatred made the air stand still. She had no will of her own. She was born to be her father's property. He was full of hate. And the little girl hated his ways. She carried love within her heart. And she created art. She made a song to prove them wrong, and then what happened would not be as bad as it was good for nothing, not as long as she made a song or a poem.

Those little victories she hid in her head and rarely talked about. That way no one could mess it up or take it away from her.

Day in and day out, she was living in fright, all alone in her prison cell in hell. She was destined to live to tell. In the meantime, she tried to be good in those mean times. Cold-hearted beatings from the man with the iron fist. He handed her bruises and memories of a life in risk. A living hell, she could tell that her virginity was already taken when she entered first grade—first grade and a few hours of getaway from the haunted house, her haunted home. She did her very best. Only perfect was nearly good enough for the devil. Driven by hatred, she delivered. She can remember how she lost contact with her body. Her mom and dad twisted her hands and twisted both her arms. They divided her wholeness by pressure to her joints. Being disconnected from herself, she stopped drawing, could not feel her own fingers. They were twisted away from their original position. She would turn cold, never thought she would get very old. And here she is this very day. She cried her pain away and is finally releasing all her disappointments. Post-traumatic stress disorder and panic attacks were what the devil ordered so many years ago. She is now thirty-five and stronger than ever before. And in her mind is a wish for the best for the rest.

IN DETROIT STARTING
MY WRITING

I sit in a motel room in Detroit. It is quiet. This is where I start writing my story. I hear the sound of the fan; it keeps me warm. The snow outside looks pretty and innocent. I watch TV, daytime gossip; it is nice to hear someone talk when I am by myself, soothing my nerves in a city I do not know. I pray to my Father in heaven, He who has always been there in my life giving good influence in my upbringing and guidance in a tried life, my guiding conscience. I came here because M&M lives here in Detroit. I admire his determination and his strength. This is the place I chose to soothe my nerves and gain some perspective at this point in my life. It is almost Christmas, and this is my gift to myself. Without my nerves, I can't go very far in any directions. I don't like secret advice and manipulation or guiding hands from an unknown source—except from God, that is. I got my fair share of that many years ago. And so here I am in Detroit, the broke city. So am I, so we kind of go together in a way. At least this is where I will start to tell my story, from my memory and my experiences, to let it off my chest and let it go. Hopefully, by telling this story, I can help someone out there overcome their obstacles too.

ABOUT CHILDHOOD

I know that a childhood is something most people remember with joy, laughter, protection, freedom, and safety. The story can be slightly different when you grow up with a predator and his wife. The two people who put you into this world are the ones you fear the most. I would say that if God was not in my life, I would not have been here today. Because in darkness, surrounded by the enemy, the world of madness could easily be your lifelong dwelling place. But God wanted it differently for me. Why? Still I am not sure of that question. All I know is that twenty years of my life has been actively devastated by the enemy, and the rest of it I have tried to cope with my wounds. My name is Ruby Lee—the name means "a warrior in battle" and was given to me by my grandfather. He died the year that I was born, but before he died, he said, "If this is a girl, name her Ruby Lee." I grew up in Norway, born in Stavanger. I have two siblings, an older sister and a younger brother. My mother still lives in Norway and my father just recently passed away.

A CHILD IS A NEW PERSON

E very child is born with his or her own potential and its own personality. If you give the child the boundaries, correction, explain things to them, give them good routines, let them know they are loved for who they are, support their personal growth, and teach them to live, then the child will grow up to be a content version of itself. Remember, children have never before lived in this world, and they need you, their parents, to guide them in a loving way toward their own ability to stand on their own two feet in this world. They need you more than ever in these tried times we all live in. Traumas and bad experiences change you in a sick way. You may think that arguing with your husband or boyfriend loudly around the children does not affect them because they are so small. Well, it does change them. You put fear into their system. You bring nervousness and insecurity into their growth, and they carry this along their life as an unwanted bump in their trust. Everybody has disagreements, but that is different from yelling and screaming. I was born an artist. I loved to perform. I loved to write poems. I loved to paint. But most of all, I loved to sing. I loved music. I was happy, and I liked sharing my happiness with my surroundings. I started in a theater for children, took painting lessons, and started to play the piano, but I quit these activities just as fast as I started them because of a high anxiety level. Communist people don't like arts. And I most definitely grew up in a communist family. I remember losing my ability to use my hands, being terrified twenty-four hours of the day, and the silence—thin, sharp, and cold silence. I was naturally born a happy child. I liked to sing and make little performances. I had no fear connected to either. That was from the beginning. But you see, the devil doesn't like music. He doesn't like dancing either. And he doesn't like jokes and happy comments. He is ruthless and with no compassion whatsoever. He uses his physical force to get his will done. And he does whatever pleases him, with no concern of whatever happens with the people surrounding him or how it affects their emotions or perceptions of the world. They are, to him, his property and his workforce. I wrote a song, "A Child's Voice," a long time ago, and in it I say, "It is your birthright to be respected as a child." And it really is your birthright to be respected as a child!

THE HAUNTED HOUSE, MY HOME

My father was the chief of the house, and my mother his little puppet. I, my sister, and my brother were merely there to help with his needs. I had little or no contact with neither my sister nor my brother. The house we lived in was a haunted terror house, and I get a fearful feeling just by thinking of that place. The atmosphere in there sent chills down my spine, and it was as if there was a presence of something unseen in it. Unseen, always present and frightening. A friend of mine said, "Whenever I would sleep over there, I was scared to death." I did not have too many visitors there. I had to sleep there every night. Yes, it hurt. I was afraid all the time. The house was a torture building to me. I had to enter against my will. It had a nice facade and was placed in a nice area. People lived easy lives and had food and houses. I would say it was a middle-class area. The house consisted of three floors: the basement, the middle floor, and the attic. When you entered our home, you would come into a wind-catcher area with a glass door into the rest of the house. Trying to catch the wind in windy surroundings. The house had a little room right next to the entrance, my little brother's room. And straight ahead of the entrance was my parents' room facing to the back of the house with no other outlook but the sea. From my parents' room, you could enter a bathroom, both from the hallway and the room. Next to the room was the stairway up to the second floor, and around the corner was a glass wall and a glass door parting the living room from the stairs and the rest of the house. Just before you entered the glass door, you would see a stairway down to the basement. The kitchen you could enter both from the hallway and the living room. It was a tiny kitchen with windows facing the yard in front of our house. The garage and the parking lot in front kept the whole view quite sheltered from the street and other people. From our big living room windows, all you could see was the sea. I'd hide between the curtains and the sea more than once, with my eyes closed hoping to survive one of the many, many attacks. When you walked upstairs to the attic the stairs were open and your feet could be seen from the living room. At the end of these stairs, you came to a small hallway, still visible from the downstairs. To the left of the end of the stairs was my room, and to the right of the end of the stairs was my sister's room. It was impossible to walk between the rooms without having the eyes of the devil catch us, pointing us back to where we belonged, in our little prison cells. In this hallway was a tiny door leading into the attic—a place where my mother would break all my trust concerning unconditional love, leaving a big gap in the heart of a child.

Walking into my room you could see the attic on your right hand side. Straight ahead were five big closets with red fabric on them, only two of which were mine to use. The roof was angled and where the roof angled only a little triangle of air parted the closet and the ceiling. In the room were a bed and a tiny window in the roof, also with a red fabric curtain on it. The window faced the sky, and below was the sea. This must have been very convenient for a predator. No one could hear you scream from that part of the house. Under my floor was the living room. Mostly it was filled with a deadly silence or high-pitched fights. I would crawl into the hallway more than once to see if my mother was still alive after all the yelling and screaming i heard. You see, from the open stairs, through the glass wall, you could also look into the living room. The sounds from our everyday room went right into my spine and froze me in fear. My mother would fight and scream, terror it sounded like. My brother and sister stayed in their rooms, but I would sometimes crawl out into the hallway to see if she was being murdered or not. Occasionally I would just crawl out there with my covers to sleep on the orange rug floor because my room scared me just as much as the sounds from downstairs, so if they were quiet, I would lie on the floor to feel safer. There were no safe places in that house. It was like one long war zone. A hidden enemy, sometimes direct physical personal attacks, sometimes wordy faraway attacks. It all happened inside the house. This was my home. No one knew, and no one would believe it if you told them either.

From my bed in the room, all I could see was the tiny window in the roof with a little red curtain covering the stars and the clouds. Sometimes I would climb out the window onto the roof and sit next to the chimney and dream about building my own little home up there. Next to the pipe, it would be nice and warm and far away from all the violence.

STARTING SCHOOL

On my first day to school, I was in a state of shock. I didn't know what school was, and so with my lack of experience, I had no idea about what could possibly happen there. I would refuse to wear a dress. I was shameful of my own body already. I refused to let my hair grow. I refused to do anything that could lead me to look pretty, because pretty had shown to be dangerous to me. I did not want to increase the danger of being abused by predators. If I attracted them to me by being cute or pretty, they would probably abuse me, which was what life had taught me up till then. Besides, my body felt trashed and parted, dissolved in a way. It was broken from beatings and from the twisting of my arms, kicking, strangling, and sexual abuse. I was in such a shock after being molested that I would just do what I was told, and I felt frozen by fear inside. I could not sit straight, and still to this day, I have trouble sitting straight. I am soon to be thirty-five years of age and have spent five, going on my sixth year, trying to fix these damages. Each and every day, I have been in my home, working on muscle by muscle in order to release the tensions and be movable again. My shoulder was out of its position, and the pain in my back was so severe that six years ago, I was no longer able to lift the guitar off my shoulders. The pain would just knock me over completely, and I could hardly lift the arm. I had to support it with the other arm in order to write and do things with it. My whole life I had suppressed these pains, and they sure came back to haunt me later on. But school was a nice getaway for me, and at the end of the day, I resisted going home.

School is a blur, and I only remember that I liked it because people were nice there and I could get away from my home for a few hours. Now I really feel like stopping the writing, going through the house really got to my nerves, but I can't. I need to continue writing because I have to get it out. I have carried these secrets on my heart my whole life and I have to pause my writing and cry a little because it is emotionally draining going through all these memories. I refuse to quit though, because I know that in a few hours, I will be satisfied with the work I have done. Writing this book releases a huge amount of suppressed emotions, and many times during my writing have I thought about quitting. But I didn't, and now I am proud of it. So if you have traumas to work through, don't ever quit—no matter how long it takes, don't ever quit! Because you will eventually get through it. I promise, you will eventually get through it. And when you get through it, the strong immediate emotions will let go and you can continue living with the memories, not the actual incident. The work I did in school and the teaching also got my head out of the darkness that it was in. And also when I started school, I had not ever been asked "How are you?" "What would you like to do?" "Did you like this or that?" "How do you feel?" These were questions that simply did not occur in my home life. Therefore, I did not ever consider it either, and therefore, I don't know. And when anyone outside our home asked me, I found no answers for them because I felt terrible inside and I just wanted to cry, and in order to be able to cope, I could not ever talk about anything that went on behind closed doors. It took me thirty five years to get out of Norway into USA to learn to talk about these things in a sober condition.

My place of getaway, my place of consistency. I placed many of my years there, twenty years of school altogether. I have taken child and adolescent care, English, music, and teaching school. I was in my third year of teaching school when I almost got killed at my job, I got in an unhealthy relationship, I wrote my bachelor paper, and i headed for my breakdown, because you will have a breakdown if you never address your emotional wounds.

THE DREAM

When I was around eight to nine years of age, or maybe earlier, I had this reoccurring dream that kept haunting me for a long time. It still is vivid in my memory, and I still recall the fear that this created in my childhood world. There were no one to talk to or get comfort from. Dreams are messages from the subconscious mind, and they are of importance when they reoccur. It can be helpful to take a closer look at the symbols in your dream if it keeps reoccurring.

"Ruby Lee, Ruby Lee," a whispering voice so tempting and horrifying that it froze me completely called my name. I did not want to look at the voice, but I could not resist turning my head because the voice was so silent and so persistent. I was seated in the backseat of the car. We were driving. The sun was shining, and my sister and brother were there. A normal day, a normal situation. But this voice kept whispering my name insistently, forcing me to look. I turned my head around, and there was no window behind me. No view whatsoever, as a matter of fact, only darkness—a never-ending, endless darkness. I screamed as I woke up with my eyes wide open in the dark, and turned on the light. It was just a dream. No one heard me scream. And I would lie awake the rest of the night from the fear that awoke me. Then I had to get up and get ready for school. I just got in my clothes, ate, walked to school, and sat there till I had to go home. Ate. Then with the door open to try and catch a gleam of light into my room, I tried to close my eyes to get some sleep.

"Ruby Lee, Ruby Lee, Ruby Lee," the whispering voice, so tempting and horrifying that it froze me completely, called my name. I did not want to look at the voice, but I could not resist turning my head. I was seated at my desk in school. The teacher was speaking, trying to keep the attention, and my fellow students and I were there, trying to hear what she said. It was a normal day, a normal situation. And then this voice came back. Its whisper was strongly hypnotic, and it kept whispering my name insistently, forcing me to look. I turned my head around, and there were no shelves there, no fellow students, and no view whatsoever, as a matter of fact, only darkness—a never-ending, endless darkness. I screamed, my eyes were wide open in the dark, and I turned on the light. It was just a dream. No one heard me scream. And I would lie awake the rest of the night from the terror that awoke me. Then I had to get up and get ready for school. I just got in my clothes, ate, walked to school, and sat there till I had to go home. Ate. Then with the door open to try and catch a gleam of light into my room, I tried to close my eyes to get some sleep.

"Ruby Lee, Ruby Lee, Ruby Lee, Ruby Lee," a whispering voice, so tempting and horrifying that it froze me completely, called my name. I did not want to look at the tempting, whispering voice, but I could not resist turning my head. I was playing with my friends. We were outside playing by the sea. We created our little doll homes in between the rocks. I loved to play with Barbie dolls. The wind was blowing in my hair, and I could hear the voice of my friend. It was a normal day. We had a good time, a normal situation. And then this voice came back. Its whisper was strongly hypnotic, and it kept whispering my name insistently, forcing me to look. I turned my head around, and there was no sea there, no friendly voice, no wind in the hair, and no view whatsoever, as a matter of fact, only darkness—a never-ending, endless darkness. I screamed as I woke up, my eyes were wide open in the dark, and I turned on the light. It was just a dream. No one heard me scream. And I would lie awake the rest of the night from the terror that awoke me. Then I had to get up and get ready for school. I just got in my clothes, ate, walked to school, and sat there till I had to go home. Ate. Then with the door open to try and catch a gleam of light into my room, I tried to close my eyes to get some sleep.

"Ruby Lee, Ruby Lee, Ruby Lee, Ruby Lee, Ruby Lee," a whispering voice, so tempting and horrifying that it froze me completely, called my name again and again. I did not want to look at the tempting and pulling voice, but I could not resist turning my head. I was in the bathroom, brushing my teeth mechanically, on alert. It was a normal day, a normal situation. And then this voice came back. Its whisper was so strongly hypnotic, and it kept whispering my name insistently, forcing me to look. I turned my head around, and there was no wall there, no door, and no view whatsoever, as a matter of fact, only darkness—a never-ending, endless darkness. I screamed, my eyes wide open in the dark, and turned on the light. It was just a dream. No one heard me scream. And I would lie awake the rest of the night from the terror that awoke me. Then I had to get up and get ready for school. I just got in my clothes, ate, walked to school, and sat there till I had to go home. Ate. Then with the door open to try and catch a gleam of light into my room, I tried to close my eyes to get some sleep.

"Ruby Lee, Ruby Lee, Ruby Lee, Ruby Lee, Ruby Lee, Ruby Lee," a whispering voice, so tempting and horrifying that it froze me completely, called my name again and again and again. I screamed and turned on the light, chasing the shadows away. I cried, and my whole body was shaking. I cried in silence all the way from my soul, out the window, into the starlit night. By the grace of God, He must have held his arms around me and helped me through the night. In the morning hours I collapsed from exhaustion and got a tiny bit of rest and sleep. Then I had to get up and get ready for school. I just got in my clothes, ate, walked to school, and sat there till I had to go home. Ate. Then with the door open to try and catch a gleam of light into my room, I tried to keep my eyes open and never close them.

This dream kept reoccurring, and within two to three months, this dream kept haunting me and forced its way into all my daily life activities. I walked around in a silent state of mind, captured in a world of fear in my dreams and also in my daily life surroundings.

Some time went by, and I did not have the dream anymore. Then one day, when I had gone to sleep under my light, under the window in the roof, I had a different dream around the same subject. I still vividly remember these dreams, and therefore, I know that they are of importance. Usually you lose memories of dreams quite easily.

I was walking up the stairs in the house. I went through the door in my room, and to the right, next to the attic, was my bed. I reached over my bed and put my finger on the switch and shut down the electricity to my playground cabin that was in our backyard. When I switched, my surroundings changed, and I found myself crucified in the same darkness I saw in my dreams. And the voice was faceless in the dark, calling my name in its intense whisper. The voice was shooting burning arrows at me. And when the arrows hit my chest, I woke up gasping for air.

This last dream with the voice in it kind of made a shift in my reality. I had no memories of the mentioned attacks anymore. They lived in my body but not in my memory. It would take me twenty-five years to be able to cope with the brutality of the truth. It was as if God came into my life and wiped away the memories of my past. After this, I just moved along with my heart closed, driven by hatred toward the devil and his followers. Full of shame and fear locked down in my mind somewhere, I just started, in silence, to do everything I was told. And I did it well, without complaints and no tears, just focused on the commands I was given. I was driven by hatred and an attitude of never giving in to this evil teaching. He would knock me over the face so I flew through the room. I learned to deal with these beatings, and so after a while, I fell to the ground, and I would just get back up on my feet and look at him without a word. I was too numb and too horrified to react.

THE ATTIC AND MOTHERLY
BROKEN TRUST

I found no use in telling anyone because my mother would only be mad at me and wipe me off like an annoying piece of trash. Just to spare myself the humiliation, I kept my mouth shut. I thought other people would also react in the same manner as my mother did. People from outside this hell-held institution they called a family would most certainly not have the ability to understand the terror that lived inside this little girl. On the outside, she looked quiet and shy, not terrified and ashamed. I made an attempt to talk about it out of a devastating state of fear, and my mother was shouting at me, "Now you listen to me!" I felt guilty of having her feel so upset by trying to talk about my problems, so therefore, I went along with her to check on some things in the attic. You had to bow down when entering the little door in the wall. It was pitch-dark in there. While I was still in there, she closed the little lightbulb on the wall, and then she closed the little door. I was left in the dark repeatedly saying, "Open the door, open the door, open the door," my voice getting louder and louder, higher and higher in pitch, and my eyes, absolutely wide open, rolling back into my head. I looked over to my right, and in the darkness, I saw something darker than the dark coming at me, and as I put my arms over my head, this something came into my right side. I saw stars and fainted.

After that, nothing ever—until now, writing in this moment—became the same. I could no longer hear what people said to me. I said "What?" It was like having a cotton ball around my head and the sound could not reach my ears. My mother never mentioned this incident again. Her knowledge of what she had done and the consequences of her action was of such a character that a mother would never admit to it. I would keep away from people after this and situated myself away from them whenever there was a gathering. By myself, I felt safer, and I did not have to listen and not hear and be judged and made fun of because of that as well. She would send a weird look, like a "Yeah, I know" type of stare to people who wondered why I sat there by myself, and she would say, "You just leave her to herself. There is something wrong with her, you know." It absolutely broke my heart, and I started to hate everything they both did. I wrote a poem at this moment in time, and I still have the original with my handwriting. Here it is; I proudly present it twenty seven years after the words came together.

The Art of Smiling

The art of smiling is the art of laughter.
Practice crying and maybe you'll make it.
The art of the heart is the art of everything.
If you lose your heart, you lose everything.
I lost my heart
And I lost everything.
Now I lie dead
Buried in a coffin under the ground
Soon to be entering/changing [I can't see which one
because I erased and rewrote it.]
Gods land.

I would act in the opposite way of what I saw and refuse to be a part of that evil behavior they taught me. I could not believe that this was going to be my home till I could move out and live by myself. I was just a child, but still I knew that this place was hell on earth. And I saw years and years ahead of me where I had to live there because I knew that a child could not move out by its own. I learned early that there were opposites of everything. And I figured that if it was possible to be this sad, it was also possible to be just as glad. I knew the sorrow in my heart, and yet I saw the smiling faces on other people. Therefore, I drew the conclusion that it had to be possible to be just as glad as I felt sad. And this joy is what I have been searching for my whole life. If people from outside my home had not told me different things about me than I was told within my family, I would have completely lost my mind. And in a way, I also did.

DISAPPOINTMENT OF "OUTSIDE PEOPLE" AND "INSIDE PEOPLE"

L ater I learned to cope with the disappointment of "outside people" because they did not have the knowledge or the fantasy, thank God, to understand or even imagine the true horror of the situation. That tells me that this is a special scenario, far from the reality other people face. But you don't know that when you are a child. Still, it has always been an essence of safety in the fact that if no one knew the story, then they would treat me normally. You see, when something like this is your story, your home, you can't really talk about it because if you were to talk about it, everything that you contain would just burst out and lead to breakdown everywhere. And that would make it almost impossible to live with the traumas, and people would not understand or wish to be told because they did not know what to do and everybody was afraid of my father. And when you are frozen in fear, you kind of just wish for whatever routine you become a part of. Because on the inside, you try and cope with so many broken dreams, terror experiences, traumas, and disappointments. I wrote a song:

Little boy is looking out to the world with eyes filled with
sorrow. He's been waiting for years to meet a nice day
tomorrow, with tears streaming down.

Your face is pale as if it has never seen the sunlight
shining. You look around to see if anyone is minding,
little boy.

Your body looks weak as if it has never lifted a finger.
You try so hard not to show anyone you linger, with tears
streaming down.

My songs always mirror something from within my own experience,
but I rewrote it a little bit in order to disguise what was really going
on inside. You get threatened so much that you honestly believe that
you will be killed if you choose to tell. Due to my own experiences,
I grew a strong bond with everyone who was being mistreated and
treated unfairly, and still to this day, I will always stand up for the
weakest. After seeing a missionary film sent to us from my uncle in
Africa, I strongly identified with the children in the movie. Only
that I felt they were more unfortunate than me because they did not
have food and looked so hungry. So therefore, I wrote poems about
them—in Norwegian, that is. And also I collected some money and
went to the paper and took a picture, and they sent the money to
starving children in Africa. In my songs and poems, I said a lot of
things that correlated with my reality. I was quieted down a lot—as
if no one wanted to listen to my pleading prayer. To me, it was a
double betrayal, because they did not even know about my pain, but
also they did not like my writings, and I thought my writing was bad.
But in the afterthought, I guess it was an emotional thing. Maybe
they did know the truth, and the song made them feel something
uncomfortable, so they turned their head away from it instead of
approaching it. And that is how the outside world also became a
disappointment to a child with only a limited view. My father knew
that I sang, and so he would sometimes put me on the spot and have
me perform for his visitors. He liked it only when he could brag about

it. One day he told me to play the piano and sing; I would sing this song I wrote. Here it is:

War

It's early morning.
Still I wander around in the darkest light.
People die, people kill, people rape, and people cry.
It's all over me.
It's all over you.
You hear about it, see it, every day.
What do you do?

Once I heard somebody say,
"I don't care.
It is so far away.
I have a job, I go to work, I have a life, and I sleep at night."
Conscience in, conscience out.
Where is your humanity?
How can you eat,
How can you sleep,
When children are murdered blind?
In a country far away, there is war today.
In a country far away, there is war today.

I sang this song, and there was not a sound for a little while. Then my father tried to joke it off and started talking about something else. I don't think I ever saw those people again. And that was my experience of "outside people"—if you told, you never saw them again. And I guess that is the same experience I now have with "inside people." They want to hold on to the shame to protect the family name. Being persecuted from your own family because you want to tell the truth hurts very much, because you know that they know, and how can they then say that it did not occur when they know? I don't know, but my sister came to Nashville to testify against me in the court of law. I looked straight at her, and she could not even look me in the eyes. She knew she was lying, but my father had such a grip on us that I can sort of understand that she "had no choice" but to do as he told her. I don't know. It was wrong, though! She said, "You need to institutionalize yourself." I responded, "You can go and institutionalize yourself and take Judas [my brother] with you." I started to talk about the molestation and everything that went on in our house and that was clearly too much for her to handle. She told me to put myself into an institution. My brother said he ought to have cut the tongue off from me. They both want to hold on to the family secrets, and they are both, this very moment, in charge of the inheritance after my father. They puzzle the papers and mend the law, lying to me straight to my face as if I am incapable of noticing it. I have been taking care of my illness, consequences from my life, which is why I did not have the strength to pursue this matter. Greed is a corruption of the soul, and I have worked too hard to let something like money come in the way of the healing of my wholeness. Somehow I believe that God is good, and I am going to make it no matter what they do. My sister is terrified of me telling about the sex that went on in our house when we were children, because of her knowledge of the fact and due to her own shame, and she ought to be double shamed for the way she is acting. My brother said that I should have jumped off a bridge a long time ago considering all I have been through and with all these problems. And I can assure you that I have considered doing just that many times, but I didn't. Even inside people can let you totally down in situations like this. They are protecting their shame and guilt and, basically, just act out of keeping the facade clean. So I guess no one really wants to deal with all these things, and that makes the dark area of the predator very big. There is a silent, enormous area of possible abuse behind closed doors, which is why I choose to be totally open about what went on in our home. Besides, people need to take responsibility for their own actions. And people need to know. And you can't just shut down the victim just to protect the madness of the predator. This goes on not only within my family but in society as a rule, and a lot of people out there suffer in silence. And I can assure you that there are *many* closed doors around our heads this very day.

MY CONDITION AFTER THE
DREAM AND THE ATTIC

Well, I went along with my little life after the dreams I had. I can't really explain how, but I just walked around as a fear-frozen zombie, trying to cope with my surroundings. And if anyone tried to touch me, I would scream, kick, and just hit furiously around me. That was how I got my father to stop violating my body sexually. And that was also the time when the humiliation really started to bloom in the home. I was so freaked out by all that had happened that I would be terrified no matter what they wanted me to do. So I made many mistakes—spilled things and bumped into things and said things out of order. And they would look at me as a piece of entertainment and gather around and just laugh at me. I was turned into a victim, a scapegoat, and a laughingstock. My numbness was a breath of relief for the predator and his wife, I guess, because in such a state, I was not able to tell anything really. There were too many secrets beaten into, broken down, and kept inside that little body. I guess their plan for my future was for me not to have one or do to me as they did my grandmother—put her into a mental institution and visit politely as the caring couple. They were also careful on how they acted around other people; the minute other people left our presence they would show the real deal and change faces. But they acted politely around other people and could even be seen as very friendly.

METHODS OF PUNISHMENT

I was a quiet child in my home. Once when I spoke my heart, my father would grab hold of my tongue and pull it out of my mouth. Simultaneously, he would grab my face and push it in the opposite direction. It hurt, and it made no sense to me why he would treat me like that. My face was trashed many times during the years. I was a talkative child when I was at my friend's house further down the street. I would talk to her parents about my secret life because they would actually listen. I did not talk about the terror. I just talked about the things I liked to do. By my secret life, I mean my emotions, my likes and dislikes, my own daily life experiences. Because when I was in my home, I would be ignored or laughed at when I tried to talk. Or they would just start talking in the middle of my stories and silence me out. My friend did not know this, so she would be mad at me for only talking to her parents when I was there, kind of felt left out, I think. It was difficult though to try and remain normal in any situations because of my shock treatment and the heavy brutal molestation I had already been through. My body was greatly violated from before I reached the age of five, penetrated and devastated and getting no protection from a mother. But these things

I forgot, and I did not remember them until much later, almost thirty years later. In that period, my life consisted of repeated patterns. I would pass out, be raped, wake up, and feel shame again and again and again, without the slightest clue of why or of what to do. On the outside, it was hard to see all this. The command in the house was to never talk about any of this, and therefore, you also learn to keep quiet about it elsewhere. It has lead to a huge amount of "MizzUndaStandings" in my life. This is the name of one of the songs I recorded on my album "*...butAlive!!!*" I think I scream, but there ain't no sound.

My father could knock me over with his iron-armored fists. But after enough beatings, you develop a protection, so after too many of those, I would just look at him in silence and get back up on my feet. I think I scared him; he did not understand my behavior. I was wounded, so I just spent all my time looking at him, everything he did. I watched without a word, not a sound. A study of the predator, I was trying to read his performance, with my poker-broken-face and no choice. You can't move out on your own as a child. He beat my face so hard on both sides—with his fists that he wiped the smile off from my face. Literally, my muscles were numbed into silence. He would come from behind and grab my neck so hard that I went down on my knees, and it numbed my ability to move. He did this many times and probably took away some of the connections to the rest of my body. He would grab my arms and twist them out of alignment in my shoulders. He would pinch my joints to such an extent that he disabled me from moving properly and disconnected my muscles and numbed them down. I sat like a broken toy, hanging over on my right side. At the age of four or five, he violated me / raped me. I passed out from the pain and the nausea, cold sweating, and terrible pain. He completely violated me, deforming me and leaving a big gap in my body and my soul before the age of five. I could not sit on my butt anymore, and my lower back was also out of alignment. My hip was pushed back and my foot out of its normal position. I can't even remember how I learned to live with that. I don't even know if it is possible to live with that, but I do know my memory vanished after the dreams and that is why I think it is of God. Something beyond our human understanding helped me live with this till I was able to cope with the reality. My mother knew about the abuse, but she chose to completely overlook it. When I tried to talk to her, all she said was, "How can you go along with something like that?" So she basically blamed it on me. Later I understood that this was jealousy from a mother, which came as a complete surprise to me because in my mind, it is highly abnormal to be jealous of your own offspring.

One time, I did speak against his behavior even if I knew that if I said something, I would be punished severely. He did something to my brother, and I was very protective of him because I loved him and tried to make his life a little bit better. So I did say something against the treatment, and after I said something, I immediately ran up the stairs to my room and hid in my bed. He came after me and grabbed me by my ankles. He pulled, and I held on to the railing of the bed. He pulled with full force while I tried with my force to hold back. It twisted my body out of alignment, and he pulled me down to the bathroom. He sat on the toilet and pulled my pants down and laid me over his knees. With his leather belt he whipped or whopped (whatever you choose to call it) me many times, and he wasn't playing. Nor was my lower back spared—it was whipped into tensions—tensions I still try to get out my back today. Crushed by sorrow and pain and with no mother to comfort me, I was just put into my bed and left there to learn not to be disobedient. God must have heard my cries and protected me from losing my mind.

A lack of touch in your life erases the reception of the outside world to an extent. So at this point in my life, I am trying to feel the outside from the inside again. And also a lot of abuse makes you not want to be home in your own body, and spiritually, you can actually move out. When no one touches your skin except when they beat on it, the biggest organ of the body, the skin, is being neglected to such an extent that you actually lose your sense of physical gravity. It is like someone taking the wrapping off from something and looking right through it. You become a see-through person—a see-through person and a punching bag. As a punching bag, I highly recommend inhaling air into your abdomen so that you become like a ball. You see, if someone beats on you when you are all ballooned, they can't really punch your inner organs. So it serves as a way of protection. What may be a problem, though, is to get this back in order after many years as a punching ball. It's kind of like trying to recall breathing patterns and sucking it back toward the spine. When your spine is distorted, you also lose connection with God. You can kind of sense His being in your spine. Did you ever feel a tingling spine? My own spine has been a roller coaster from the day that I was born. It was twisted and torn, squeezed and outworn.

HANDBALL AND VICTORY

There was a period in my life where I started to do ball sports. My neighbor told me she had started playing handball, and so I said I wanted to go there too. And so I did. This was hard for me to cope with, given my body was so bruised on the inside and out of whack. But as I said, I think God wiped away the memory of my injuries, and since I had no memory of that, I just started to practice. I got my own ball. So after school, I would go over to the playground and just stand there and shoot at a wall, hour after hour after hour after hour. It was a good place to be. I was occupied in my own activity and did not have to interact with anyone, and I started to be good at it. Also, I was building a new layer of muscles that would keep me going for many years before the abuse once again started to haunt me. I scored many goals. My physique was improving, and I felt some kind of nonfailure for the first time. I never asked anyone from my home to come and see. My mother would be there sometimes and my father hardly ever. I used to go with my friends from the team. Thank God for friends and friendships. Not until later, when I was very good at it, would my father appear in the audience—only to break whatever success I was. He would sit on the opposite side from the rest of the parents with my brother. He laughed and shouted, "Go, Ruby Lee! Go, Ruby Lee!" He had my brother laughing with him and shouting out my name only, not the team, but only to humiliate me. I scored many goals, but most of all, I wanted to shoot the ball right in his disgusting face. He would appear like that on certain occasions only to stop me from succeeding in anything. He never ever asked how it went on my ball games otherwise. He just could not stand to see me succeed. His interference in my life was a devastating one. At the team, I met my best friend. She was one year older than I and my best friend since my childhood friend moved away.

HANGING WITH THE
WRONG CROWD

She hung out with the wrong crowd, her older brother and their friends. She and I began to drink. I was twelve years of age. The drinking increased as the years went by. And with the drinking, I would pass out, vomit, and fight and be raped. I had no memory after being drunk. I could just wake up somewhere without even remembering how I got there. I remember coming home to my mother's house after a night in town. My friend's older brother, ten years or so older than I, had to stay outside because my mother was home. I went inside and was relieved because I could go to bed without having to do anything I did not want to. I fell asleep and woke up several hours later by someone coming into my room. My friend's brother told me that he had been talking to my mother in the living room because she had spotted him in the garden, only to invite him in. He had told her he was an alcoholic. He was a notorious criminal, well-known in our community. After telling my mother all these things, she said to him that he could just go down to the basement. He was surprised when he told me. I was fifteen years at that time. The pain I carried inside made me feel more alike the troubled people than the ones my own age. I continued to hang with the wrong crowd for many years. It was a warning—it is a big warning sign if your child ever starts to hang with the wrong crowd because they present so many ways in the wrong directions that the child would not have been exposed to otherwise.

REPEATING OLD PATTERNS

From birth to age 5, a child's pattern is created. It is created by the child's protectors. And if a child learns healthy routines, this child will continue to follow these routines later in life. It is most crucial that you, as parents, are aware of this because you are the teachers, and whatever you teach your child at this age will be their foundation. When you give birth to a child, you give birth to a new person. This person needs you. This person will be your biggest fan for as long as you live. You have someone who finds you the most beautiful person in the whole wide world. As a mother, people seem to forget this, and the child often becomes an annoyance to the mother because the mother can't see the beauty in her that the child loves so unconditionally. This often creates a conflict. I remember writing a song to my mother from my brother and me, and it said, "We hope you love us. We hope you love us because you are so beautiful."

When a mother does not feel beautiful, she can turn her inner emotions out on the child's love for her and, therefore, undermine the child's opinion. A child will look upon you, as a father, as the strongest, bravest, and most admirable person in the whole of the world. If fathers took this into consideration, they might not run out or continue competing with fellow men in order to get this very same acknowledgment of high standing. If they only listened with their hearts and saw the unconditional love that the child has for them, they would be fulfilled as the bravest, strongest, and most admirable men in the whole of the universe. It is a child's gift to the parents. And I think that the least a parent can do is to be a gift to the child that they chose to bring into this world. Teach them healthy routines and relationships by giving them healthy routines, caring, and boundaries.

I never learned these important aspects of life, and I and my friends would go out drinking, and when we did, all my inner struggles came out in the open. By inner struggles, I mean all the suppressed emotions I carried. A lot of anger, hurt, sadness, disappointments, fears, anxiety, trauma, shock, and the list goes on and on. Basically, I feared for my life from birth till I moved twenty-five years later. At an early age, I was an easy prey for men out to hunt. I would drink to get drunk. I would get so drunk that I would pass out to create a space of some freedom from inner struggles, but when you pass out, you're an easy prey for anyone who wishes to exploit you. I was pretty, and I was an easy prey, and I did not know that. My mother never ever told me I was beautiful. I just felt disgusting and dirty, and my face had been violated and felt all twisted and weird. When a man came on to me in this condition, I was actually helpless because, subconsciously, the molesting of my body had numbed me. And my father's teaching was to obey his commands no matter what he commanded. That was how I was trained, and that was how I acted. A man was superior to me, and I had to obey his command. I ended up having sex with a lot of men from the age of twelve when I started drinking. I could not stand having sex with all these guys when I was drunk, a different man every weekend. It made me highly anxious to wake up in different locations, misused and with no memory. I kept digging myself deeper and deeper into my own shame, and I felt very guilty of being a mean and disgusting person, just like my mama told me. I was repeating a pattern without remembering the incident that led to this tragic, continuous pattern of disgrace and continuous adding to my sense of no self-worth. The sex gave me no joy or satisfaction, only shame and guilt. I was never taught that my body is a holy temple for the spirit to live in. I just kept violating it like I had been taught to do. On the weekends, my mother would give me money to get drunk. I could not take the shame I felt. My mother's accusations, looking at me as dirt, had me feel that what they had said about me all my life was actually true. My own behavior stated what they had said all along: I was stupid, ugly, mean, evil, retarded, and useless; a laughing stock and a scapegoat, a person whose body anyone could use if they wished to. "Who do you think you are? You think you are so much better than us?" The accusations came from my mother because I despised their behavior and also told them so. And when I was sober, I always treated people nice. But after my drinking started, I was convinced of their point of view, given that I was providing evidence for their judgment on my behalf due to my drunken behavior.

Before the age of twelve, I got my period. I did not know what this was, and I was continuously bleeding for maybe a month and then had two days off, and back it came again. And I was bleeding a lot—I thought I was dying. I had an older friend who took me to a doctor, and I asked for birth control pills to get this period in check. I could not speak when I was in there, so she had to talk to the doctor on my behalf; I just fought for my life not to cry. I got the pills, and I am glad I did, or else I would probably bleed to death or get pregnant at an early age. I am glad I did not have to do any of those. I also tried a hormonal sort of medicine to regulate the bleeding, but it did not work. In hindsight, I think it was life telling /showing me about the wounds that had been inflicted on me. But I did not remember the sexual abuse at this point in time.

THE END OF DRUNKENNESS
AND THE BEGINNING OF
A SPEED ADDICTION

When I tried amphetamine the first time it was given to me by the same guy that my mother served me to at the age of fifteen, I was hooked. I was too drunk to remember taking it, but what I do remember is that I slowly came back into reality from being blacked out on alcohol. I got sober again that way, and this gave me a sense of control. I was walking around for six to seven hours, talking while I brushed my teeth. There were toothpaste and words everywhere. I think he kind of regretted giving speed to me at that point in time, but he had already shown me a way to gain control of my blackouts and sexual sins. That was it for me. I finally gained a sense of control. I was seventeen to eighteen at that time. At first I would only take it when we went out drinking. But after a while, I found that it gave me energy, and I would go out to friends under influence—would sit there forever. I lost my time perspective and my inner tensions had me stuck wherever I was. And I talked a lot. And I sang. And I felt kind of free, at least from regret, and in control of my actions in that state of mind. But it tired me out, and the happy state did not last very long.

At the age of twenty-one or twenty-two, I finally found the courage to leave my mother's house. When it comes to my mother, I haven't talked to her in five or six years. And to be honest, I have not missed her even once. I am glad that she is not part of my surroundings, and I would like to keep it that way. Why? She has manipulated me so badly that I could not even take my own life because she would make me feel guilty of disappointing her. Her favorite statements were "I am so disappointed in you. I am so disappointed in you. You are evil. God, you are disgusting." She never listened. She undermined my whole existence. She expected me to be around her and take care of her. I had to soothe her and tell her how pretty she looked and make her smile. It was terrible. She made me feel so useless and disgusting, and I did not understand the double message she was sending. She would offend me first, and then she would say, "But you know I love you." She confused me so badly that she broke every little leftover of courage that I had in me. She was the reason I finally broke totally. She would call me every week, and the words she said were so disappointing that I can't even begin to describe them. It is just like spitting on someone who is so down and out that they can hardly breathe. Then they feel good about themselves when they raise someone else's feeling of uselessness. She controlled my emotions, she controlled my words, she controlled my life. It took me twenty-five years to realize that a mother could actually be jealous of her own child. To me, that is so far from common sense that it is even hard for me to imagine being jealous at a child. If I had a child, I would be so proud to see my genes and my teachings living on in another person, making that person happy and having progress in their life. Nothing would make me more proud than that, so to me, it is absolutely beyond my imagination. Someone had to tell me in straight words that my mother was jealous of me. That woman has hurt me so dearly and physically wounded me so badly that if I had the words to tell long ago, she would have been put into prison along with my father for child abuse. She twisted my left arm so badly that I just remember crying "You broke my arm. You broke my arm." And I ran away from there. I was maybe about four to six years old.

My mother manipulated me so badly she took over my life and directed how I was to feel and behave. All her own shame and guilt, she gladly poured it out on me. And she wished to keep it that way in order to keep me from telling on her, i guess. One look from her, and she goes right into my very core. I was in Bible study the other day, and I recalled a dream I had. I was sitting in the passenger seat of our car, and my mother was in the driver's seat. She was dead, and my father came running up behind the car. I had to switch over to her seat, and as I sat on her lap, I needed to remove her right foot from the gas pedal. I sat on her, and I put the car in reverse and stepped on the gas and ran over my father twice, because I put it in first gear and stepped on it again. I woke up after that. It did not make much sense to me then, but it makes more sense to me now as I am trying very hard to get out of her emotional grip on my being. She controlled my car; now I have problems understanding how I drive my car, my body. It is hard to start relating to my own emotions given they were taken from me at such an early age. I did take her foot off the pedal when I started to work on my issues. I did reverse and run over my father when I faced him in the courtroom. And I am running over him twice now that I actually do the forbidden thing in telling my story from my own experience as honestly as I can.

When I started to do amphetamines, it kept me from sleeping with a lot of men. I could keep control of my actions then. Years after I started using again, I was again reminded of the abuse I tried so hard to run from. What happened when I was in a state of an amphetamine high was that I would download tons of porn on my computer and watch it apathetically, resemblances of my own abuse kept rolling in front of my eyes, but I did not really know that at that actual point in time. But when I look back, it is clearer to me that it was my unconscious mind, my long-hidden memories, telling me to deal with long-gone memories of my own experiences of sexual abuse. I would have to deal with the underlying cause of my running, my addiction/sin, and my untold pain, or else I would die in these circumstances. I did not wish to die in such circumstances. The road back has been the hardest part, but now I am glad I have gone through the humiliating situation of recalling something as hideous as sexual abuse. You see, it is the last thing you would like to be a part of your memory and history. It makes me sick to my stomach having to think about it. But maybe by doing so will I, for once, be able to enjoy a normal and warm and touching relationship, a passionate interaction with a loving and desirable man of my taste. Other than this, I am not very fond of touching, only for a special someone. The rest can keep their hands and imaginations to themselves. I will only share myself with one person, and I believe in monogamy.

NAUSEA, SWEAT, AND FAINTING

During the first sexual attack, I passed out in pain, and the nausea that I experienced at that moment in time came haunting me later on many occasions. See, this pattern was established before the age of five: rape, passing out, and nausea. To be serious, psychologists do not joke when they say that your behavior toward your child before the age of five determines their later approaches to life. In my situation, this pattern would be to be abused and pass out without saying a word, without any comfort, without anything but shame and guilt and self-blame. My mother placed the responsibility of me being abused on my shoulders. I guess that way she knew I would never tell, and her emotions, her hurt around being the second choice of her husband, would remain untold. She would also later pay for the alcohol that I would use only to bruise my soul, pass out, and be abused by whoever was there, ready to feed on the prey.

I was standing in the bathroom, fixing my earring, when I started to feel very much unwell. I could not determine where the discomfort came from. I felt like I had to vomit or maybe use the toilet, or maybe I needed food? I could not place the feeling, but it was all in me, making me very unwell, dizzy, lose eyesight, get cold sweat, and causing me to lose balance. I started to get cold sweat, and before I could turn to the toilet, I would just black out, and I fell backward, right into the wall. The wall was too close to me, so I smashed my head right into the wall, and my neck would feel as if it was broken right between my shoulders. I woke up. Slowly sounds and smells and emotions all faded into my presence again from dark. It hurt like hell, and I could not move my head. It was stuck in that position that I hit the wall. I had peed in my pants. And I was ashamed of that; I did not want anyone to see. I would cry and cry and cry, and my mother would comfort me. But she never called the doctor, nor did she take me to a hospital. I was put on the couch and just had to go on living like that afterward. I lived on that couch for a little while, and I think that is the first time I felt like I was looked after.

I also remember being on the playground with our neighbor kids. We played baseball, and I was on a good team. Then I was to hit and felt the same nausea coming over me and started to have cold sweat. I could not place the emotion. It just filled me up, and I stumbled out of the game over to a bench. I sat down, sweating, blacked out, and fell right over on the bench. I faded back into reality, only to see my friend's faces staring at me and laughing, asking, "What are you doing?" I tried to smile and say, "Nothing."

I sat up. I did not hit my head because it was on the end of the bench, but I did pee my pants, and that probably made me more ashamed than anything. My friends told me that I had lifted my arms as if protecting myself and said "No, no, no." I just got on my feet and went home to tell my mother. I was very ashamed of it all. She found me a new pair of pants, and that was it. We never talked about it. I think I fainted on more occasions also, but I can't really remember it. My mother would say, "You need to do something with your head. You need to do something with that passing out that you're doing."

When I was eleven years of age, I was to go on a camp with my classmates. I nearly missed it because then I had a doctor's appointment. I was to go check my head. My mother said for me to go with my father. I was terrified. I lay on a bench, and this nurse came in with a shot of some kind that just seemed enormous to me. On my head they placed some kind of jelly and things stuck to my head, and I saw a picture of it in the lamp above me. It scared the hell out of me. Then the machine started to move, and I was inside some kind of a tube. I cried hysterically but had to be quiet in the machine. When I was done, my father would drive me out to the camp in our boat. I arrived later than all the others and was just afraid. From the camp, I don't really remember very much. The test never really told me anything as I remember.

I would pass out on several other occasions also. I would sit in a couch listening to music, smoking weed with some friends. I started to feel the same nausea and sweat, not understanding what was happening. Again I would utter some words, and then my head just fell to the side. I woke up with my friends slapping my face to wake me up. I just felt terribly unwell and wanted to withdraw from the whole situation. I was then living with a boyfriend. I can remember also on a different occasion in the same place where I was by myself in the morning. I was fixing to go to work, and I felt the same nausea. I walked into the kitchen and tried to make some food, but feeling worse and worse, I had to leave it. So I went into the bathroom and woke up again on the floor, fading back into reality again, all sweating, and my pants were wet. I hardly dared to call in sick because I did not want to cause trouble for anyone. I was thinking of going there, but I had to call in sick. I felt so guilty from doing that. And the day went by, and I did not talk about it. I just felt bad about it, like it was my own fault. Like there was something wrong in my head. I also remember on a different occasion, I was dating a guy, and he and I and one more couple had gone away for the weekend to a cabin. We were playing cards, and I tried to cope. Then I started to feel unwell, and I went outside for a cigarette. On my way back inside, I passed out in the hallway. I faded back into reality and just felt very much ashamed of the situation. I borrowed my friend's jogging pants—I wet my pants, and I felt so guilty when I told her about it.

The rest of the stay, I can't really say I remember much from. On a different occasion, I was at the Roskilde Festival. It was a fun time until I went to buy myself some food. I started to feel nauseous and sweating again, and I passed out right on the grass. I woke up with ten heads staring at me, paramedics also. But I said I was doing fine and got up on my feet and walked, hurried away from there. When I told my mother about it, she said, "You need to go and check on your head. You need to do something with that head of yours." I remember waking up in the shower. I remember waking up on the toilet, just falling like a rag doll. I did pass out on other occasions, also but it is like a blur to me. I now realize that I was repeating a pattern from the very first abuse. I just did not remember the abuse at this point in time, but I think, as I am writing, that it was the emotions that were stirred up that caused me to relive the sexual attack so many times. And also, it is life trying to tell me about the underlying cause of the fainting.

FAMILY VACATIONS

Over to family vacations. You know how it is when you come back from summer holiday and you have to write an assignment on your summer memories? Well, that was a task I slightly resented. Because here is one holiday just to give you a picture of what happened. So we were out in our boat, on an island all by ourselves, of course. So my sister and I were sitting in the front of the boat, reading comic magazines. My father was sitting in the middle of the boat, drinking whiskey and ice and listening to country music. He was talking to himself or grunting or whatever you call those sounds. The vibration was a scary note. I was aware of his increasing anger. I heard him say, "Shit in hell, I am son of a bitch." I was a Christian and believed in God, so I highly resented what he had said. My sister and I were sitting there, grips tightening on the magazines, pretending to focus on reading. Then he burst out and put his drink down, came toward us, grabbed hold of our comic books and also the rest from the table, and he just opened the window in the roof and threw all our magazines out on the sea, and then he returned to his drink and his country music. I can't really remember how we got out on shore, but I think we actually sat there for a long time, absolutely without a sound, before we silently walked by him and out to the side of the boat, hurrying toward shore, both of us terrified. I went over to my mother and told her that my father was in the boat, cursing and drinking, and I told her it was not okay that he threw our magazines out on the sea. She said she would go talk to him and walked onto the boat. It took about one second for him to lose his freaking mind, and he was yelling so loud you could probably hear him on the other side of the shore. She started screaming too. And he grabbed her by the shoulders and pushed her out on the back of the boat. There was an iron support railing there, and he held his knee into her belly and actually started to bend her over the railing. She screamed and she screamed and threw her arms in the air. I was situated on the shore, and I saw this craziness going on and thought, *Oh no, now I have killed my mother.* She managed to get out of the grip and walk out on the side of the boat. He tried to grab her legs and throw her out to the magazines on the sea, but she managed to hold to the railing with her hands and came over to us. We were all very much startled at this moment in time, and she suggested for us to go into the little boat to escape from him. And so we did, all four of us gathered in a little boat about fifteen meters from the big boat. Now that fueled up the old bastard, him being afraid of what we would do to him. My mother could not take us over to the other side of the shore because it was inhabited by his family, and she could not go there and tell them about him for this reason. So we just stayed there in the boat for hours and hours. And the freak on shore surely was a sight when he found his binoculars and hid behind a stone watching us. I laugh about it now because, hello, here is family freak on tour. It was tragic, and it colored me for many years, but since I survived it, I can finally laugh about it also. Then after hours on the water, he finally disappeared and was quiet long enough for us to go back into shore again. He had fallen asleep in the bed that I shared with my brother. I don't know why we did not all sleep together in the front of the boat, but I guess we were all so drilled that only my mother and brother would sleep in the front while my sister and I had to sleep right over from where he was at. And my sister slept with her head away from him, but I had to sleep with my head facing his head, only about a short meter apart. I did not sleep very well that night, constantly fearing another attack. So I fell asleep out of exhaustion. Then the creepiest part happened in the morning when I got up for breakfast. I was seated where I usually sat and witnessed everybody being all happy and bright and having a good morning and everything. Not a word was uttered about the event that took place the day before. What I wrote on that summer assignment, I cannot tell because this memory blurred out all the rest for a while in time.

Another day on the sea, on a different location and different vacation but still…I was pulled out of my bed in the early hours, and it was still dark outside. My father had put a fishing net on a little rock in the middle of the sea, and a storm that came in was threatening to destroy the net, so he put me into the little boat, and we took off. I was terrified already. When we came to where the net was, he could not get ahold of it due to very high waves, and so he told me to jump over onto that rock in the sea. I said, "No, I don't want to," and I started to cry. He screamed so loud that I feared him more than to drown in the sea. So I stood there on the little boat, and I was sure that I was going to drown in the dark heavy waves, but I jumped right into my death. I didn't have a choice. I actually landed on the rock, and by God's grace, I managed to free the net and get it back into the boat safely. To this day I really don't understand the outcome of many situations I have encountered. What I do know is that I would not be here today if it wasn't by the grace of God.

On another vacation, we were at a rest place along the road in our camping wagon in Poland, and my father had made grits. Well, I can tell you that the milk in Poland was slightly different from the milk in Norway. The grits tasted just like old vomit, and all three of us kids sat around the table and cried and cried trying to eat the food. I tried to say something, and he screamed like only the devil can scream and forced us to eat. Finally, I dared to say, "Taste it yourself, please. Just taste it." And he eventually tasted it, and then he threw it away.

All these horrific situations have left me with a strange kind of humor. I have developed a way to think about these things, and I see the scenario in my head without the emotions linked to it. Maybe I had cut myself off from my emotions or contained it already at that time in order to survive mentally, but today I can smile when I think about this. And so when other people tell me things that happened to them, I tend to laugh sometimes when I hear about it. It's not because I find it funny. It is because I see the scenario in my head and don't really link my emotions to it. And I don't know how this actually affects people. I may have hurt a lot of people that way, and I am sorry if I did.

We used to go camping too, and in our tiny camping wagon, you would risk getting beat up if you used too much toilet paper, because he had to empty the toilet tank. Also, if you used too much water, you would risk a beating or squeezing of your face or arms or ears. The tension created in a little camping wagon like that is just unbelievable. And the space you have to live in is close to nothing. Everything can be heard, and everything is within reach almost. The beds we had to sleep in were tiny for one person, but still, one night, my father came to my bed and was going to sleep with me, which made no sense because there was no room in there.

I lay on my side trying not to breathe, not to move a single muscle, trying not to touch him or be near him at all. It was a long night. I did move my hand, though, and accidentally touched his penis, and I said, "What is that?" and squeezed it a little bit. It made him furious, and for the rest of the night, I did not move. Silent in the presence of time takes a long time when you have to hold your breath and don't feel and don't move.

CLEANSING THE AIR ON A STUDY TRIP TO YORK

People are people no matter what their age. I was in my early twenties when I studied English in school. We all went on a school trip to York, and in the evenings, we all went out and grabbed a few beers. There was a retired man among us, and he would buy the girls a lot of beers and drinks. They didn't seem to mind this until, well, some felt he became a little too friendly. And after one of our classes, we were standing in a group of maybe thirty students, both genders, and the old man came falling out of a pub in the distance. We all saw him, and I was waiting for him when I heard some of the people say, "Oh no, here he comes," and everybody started mumbling, and then the whole group started walking away. I was the only one who stood there and waited. When everybody turned to walk away, I could hardly believe what I saw. I said, "Are you leaving him? Seriously?" I looked at the group in a shocked surprise, and they were somewhat ashamed. I said, "Well, I can be with him. You just go ahead. I can wait for him." I was one of the younger ones and probably the only one who did not exploit him for drinks. Well, we all got him home safely. I talked to the teacher, and he did not know what to say or do about the accusations. And I could not have this split in the group without all parties knowing what was being said, so I went to talk to him the next day, and I told him what people were saying about him. I also said, "I don't think your wife is very proud of you at this moment in time." I said this with care in my voice. I knew he had lost his wife a year before, and I figured this was probably the core of his problem. He started to cry, and I just sat with him till he calmed down, and I gave him a hug. The rest of the stay turned out very well for all the involved parties.

It is not a crime to care, you see. And these experiences have given me so much love and meaning that I can proudly say I would do exactly the same thing all over, even if I was sick and needed care myself.

LADYLOVEREBEL

After many years of singing and making music, writings, and poems with different groups, I kind of ended up calling myself LoveRebel, a rebel in the name of love, for love, and of love. Then I changed it to LadyLoveRebel.

My mission and motto as LadyLoveRebel is "Be your own best friend, and give yourself a good hug." LadyLoveRebel is my stage persona. *Lady* because I needed to be a little more ladylike. *Love* because where I come from, love was not a part of the deal. And you have to be a *rebel* in order to break out of such devastating surroundings. *LoveRebel* because I needed to be a rebel in order to beat the evil surroundings I was born into, and love has in it the power to conquer fear. I always loved to sing, and I wrote poems and songs from when I was a child. When I was twelve years of age, we were at an Easter holiday. I met a girl there, and she played in a band, and they didn't have a singer. "I am a singer," I said. That is when I started in my first band. I had never before in my life done anything like this for my own good, but I really just loved so much to sing that I jumped at the opportunity. So that was the beginning. I sang

"We're Not Gonna Take It" by Twisted Sister, and the irony in that is now clear to me. Also, I sang "A Lonesome Cowboy, Far Away from Home," a self-composed song.

I got into a new band, a girl band, and sang there for a while. Then they all quit—they wanted to go elsewhere with their lives, but I kept the rehearsing room, and little by little, I "forced" a few friends to play in my band, Red Tears. This was in eighth to ninth grade, so I would be fifteen to sixteen. We did a few shows, and the reception was mixed. Our instructor could not believe the lyrics I wrote. He said they were meant for an older audience than ours, and I guess he was right about that. We made a demo many years ago—three songs. We all started on different schools after this, and gradually the band vanished.

I also recorded three songs in music as a chosen subject in school. It was "The Rose," "Beast of Burden," and "What If God Was One of Us?"

I started in a soul band—a big band with four girl singers and one male main vocal, brass, and the regular setup. I sang here for a while, and we did many shows. The band was named Black Rain, and older soul and rock songs were on the agenda with some newer songs mixed in there.

After this band, I started to sing backup in a Rolling Stones cover band, the Midnight Ramblers, and I loved it! I sang with them for many years, and I kept singing with them till after I moved to Oslo to pursue my own music career. I really love the Rolling Stones's music, and I loved the people in the band!

In Oslo, I met new people, and we formed a blues band, Blue 24/7, and we did some shows with that band. We also recorded a demo, "River Deep, Mountain High," "Am I a Fool?" and "Been Burned Too Many a Times."

Some of us formed a new band, Ruby Lee and Her Bees, and we did some shows as well, and the reception was good. We made a demo, "Life Is Strange," got a radio play, "Voices, Voices," and "Silver-Lining."

People loved the music. I, on the other hand, was not doing so well. I was nearly killed by a patient at my job. He held a knife to my throat and threatened to kill me. After the incident, I was just sent home. And my boyfriend died suddenly. And I had all the damage from my early life that I tried to run from. So my inner state was very difficult at this point in time. Oh, and we recorded another song as well, "Run, Baby, Run." Life *is* strange! I was, at this time, withdrawing from society, and I just suddenly quit the band that I really loved very much. I am sorry guys!

Later I met a man who became my boyfriend, a drummer from hell. We formed a band, BBBand…, and we did a few shows as a duo. We recorded a demo, "Everyone Follows." He threw me into the walls two weeks before we were headed to play in my hometown for all the locals. At this point in my life, I was hardly alive, and a breakdown also came after the show in my hometown—a show I had to do alone with my guitar. I was on penicillin for a year; my immune system collapsed. At the end of "Everyone Follows," I say, "Mind your own business. Write your own story, because I am going to bed." And yes, I was bedridden for a year. That was back in 2008. Ever since that, I have been living to recover. A new day is just another day to recover.

In 2009, I also recorded one of my songs, "Footsteps in Fairy-Tale Land," in a studio, but I was too weak to follow the project through, so I just got a raw demo from the effort, but I like it still.

I also broke my left hand in 2010, I think. I went out roller-skating and fell on my left hand and had to have surgery on it. I could hardly believe it. That Christmas, I made some handmade business cards because I figured, if you have a goal, you need to be working on it all the time to get there. And so with my one hand, I wrote business cards.

In the recovery period that followed, I recorded an album all by myself, "…ButAlive!!!" It is a collection of eleven songs, and you can hopefully hear them one day. I play all the instruments, and it is recorded under my bed on my own little recorder with eight tracks on it. I could burn CD's right out of the recorder and I had to play the songs from beginning to end on each of the instruments I used. I played guitar, bass, drums, piano and harmonica. It came together in-between panic attacks, drug abuse, doctor visits, government letdowns, and PTSD. I finished it just before I went to Nashville, and I still haven't done anything with it. I started in 2008, and I will keep one of the songs from then, "Sharing." I was done in 2013 with the last version of my own recordings of "Life Is Strange." My dream is to get into a proper studio with great musicians and to have my album recorded properly, preferably with a producer. And I have two or three albums in my head in this writing moment.

I really want to thank my brother. He gave me this opportunity. Life has kept us apart, but I still love him with all my heart. I want to thank him for giving me money to buy my instruments and my recorder and for always being proud of me and encouraging me with my singing. I recorded all the songs with his gift, and it saved my life in many ways. I dedicate it to him and all my friends in Norway for having faith in me still—you know who you are—Thank you. My brother providing me with the money and the recorder so that I could buy instruments and build myself up. Thank you.

My acoustic guitar I carried around for over ten years. It was a Takamine, four thousand dollar guitar. I miss it. I got all the instruments I wished for in various apartments along my route. Given the government had taken my money and I was too sick to work, I could not afford to buy all-new instruments, and so God gave them to me along my route. All the instruments I wished for came to me in the most peculiar places. I wanted to give them to an orphans' home that was located not too far from where I lived, but I was never able to before I left, so I just left it all behind. Fifteen years of collected music equipment I left in my apartment and it is still hard to think about that.

Anyway, after one of my shows, a lady said to me that she wished she knew more of my story before she heard my songs, and so I figured this book will explain a lot of my thinking and my behaving. I mention it here because it is closely linked to my songs, especially the teachings that I have gained throughout these years by observing myself and observing others. And maybe it can help you in your own life somehow. That way, my story will have a purpose, and I hope it does. When I was done with my recording of "…butAlive!!!", I flew to Nashville, and that was the start of a whole new era.

NOTES AND MEMOIRS FROM THE HOMELESS SHELTER IN NASHVILLE

I crash-landed in Nashville and my condition was so bad I found myself homeless on the street with no money, panicking all the time and with no further plan whatsoever. I couldn't think at all. Someone came to me and told me about Nashville Rescue Mission and I was pulling my two suitcases with velvet dresses and jewelry in it, carrying my Les Paula Gibson guitar on my back and headed for the mission a Friday night. I got off from my drug abuse, went to counseling at the sexual assault center and attended the Church of Christ. While I stayed in the homeless shelter I took notes every day concerning the condition my condition was in. I kept a journal of memoirs and here comes some of my thoughts in writing that I did at this point in time.

Oktoberfest in Nashville

Lord, I wish I had a home. There's something really weird about this place. I am tired now. We were at the Oktoberfest at Germantown. It was nice. Good music, good vibes, and good people, a lot of impressions. But I was able to breathe, and I felt joy being there among a lot of booths and food and four stages with music. I'm finally realizing the abuse that I have been through. I haven't even been living in my own body, so now when I breathe, I try and sense my lungs, my belly, my throat. I try to think about my toes, my feet, and my hands as I am writing. I truly, really want to get back into my senses, back into my physical body. And when I do, I do it to sing forevermore. "Sing for the moment," says Eminem, "Never tomorrow. The good Lord could take you away."

Surreal Surroundings in Nashville

I feel like everything around me is from a play. There's something I should have seen that I don't. I don't understand my surroundings, so instead of focusing on what I do not understand, I am going to focus on my physical presence: fingers, hands, wrists. I think there is something in the air, but right now, I just can't focus on the signs I see because my surroundings are lying to me anyways. Someone said that I had been spoken for; I hope that is M&M. I have e-mailed him for years, you see. He was my friend in the darkness because I listened to his songs, and I knew that he would relate. And here in Nashville, I have heard his music and people asking me about rap music, so I kind of feel that he is trying to reach me. If it be so, I would most certainly faint. It is a good dream in the midst of my storm anyway! My surroundings are constructed and weird. I asked my friend, "When is your boyfriend coming?" and she says, "He just went home to take a shower, and I don't know when he'll get back then." And that just reminds me of old days when I said I'll go home to take a shower and you never knew if or when I would come back. Strange! And this is just one example of many things that has been going on around me. We are—me and four older people—going to my friend's, and I think I will get some clues then to what is going on and who is behind this. I think it could be Emm, but of that I can really, truly not be sure. It is just too insane if it is. But I have seen some things that tell me that maybe it is, but in Jesus's name, is that really possible? If so, I'll be smiling from this point onward. That is for sure.

Connecting Me to My Name and My Story

So far, what have I learned? I came from a stunningly dark place with no mercy nor grace but disgrace for myself and, I guess also then, for you. But we are sisters and brothers. When you pick, you need to make good choices. So who am I? I am. But I am also Ruby Lee, thirty-four years of age. I currently live in the women's mission in Nashville. I am a survivor. I survived sexual abuse and violent domestic physical, mental, emotional, and psychological abuse. I previously refused to feel, and because of that, I had no idea of what was real. You have to feel to make it real. I am stronger than I have ever been. I have been blessed with a good voice, good looks, and strong will and determination. I have a reversibly broken body on its way back into being shipshape. (Note: What you are about to read is really the opposite of what I was feeling in that moment, but in order to take away shame and guilt, you have to turn around your thoughts on the subject. So the more you imagine, say, and write a thing, the more you are going to believe it, especially when you have feelings of shame connected to your image of your body when the emotional core feeling also is of shame. Therefore, I said the following things exaggeratedly and directly aiming for better core emotions concerning my body. After my best attempt, I put words to my body maybe for the first time. I am trying to turn around my own thoughts and feelings on this subject because I have to live here in this body. Building good self-image and self-esteem concerning the body is essential for good being. The body is the spirit's dwelling place. It is where emotions occur and the brain can work. It all happens inside the holy temple, the body. And I am creating my identity. I am, but I also have a story and a body and emotions. It all needs to work together as a whole in order to become a full person. Self-affirmation is a good way to re-build confidence.)

Regaining Love for My Body in the Shelter

In this shelter, I am blessed with routines, a bed, a blanket, and a roof to sleep under. I get three meals a day. Right now I made my bed and am waiting for supper. I feel relaxed and comfortable, a least more than before. I try and breathe deeply and continuously. I have my sword and my shield—that being my smile. I welcome the sun into my belly, and it shines into all directions at once, and it reaches far beyond my physical being. I have toes and a foot. They stabilize me when I walk, and they stretch out and relax when I lie down. I just love both my right foot and my left foot. My ankles are strong, and they connect my feet to my legs. They are flexible, and they enable me to turn and to walk smoothly, and I love both of my ankles. My right leg and my left leg go from my ankles to my knees. They are both incredible feet, and I love my legs. I can feel the front and the back. They are lovable and also connected to my knees. My knees are strong too, and the kneecap keeps my leg connected with my thigh. I love both my thighs, and they go all the way up to my hip, and on the back, they end where my butt starts. Right in the middle is my womb. It is a treasure and a pleasure. It is my vagina, and it is a good place, and only I have the authority to decide who is allowed to touch it. I love my body, and I feel relaxed and comfortable with it. It's a divine gift of pleasure and grace. And I feel thankful of being able to let go and dive into my own pleasures. It fires up the whole engine. And I can't wait to melt into loving arms and have my flesh be one with the one I care for. (Note: It is a little odd to write this, but I chose to leave it like it was written due to my healing in order to maybe help some other victim take back a natural part of a human being, naturalize something natural.)

The Courage to Heal

Healing Begins Here, it says on the wall at the sexual assault center. I cried rivers the first time I was there. I cried from the parking lot, throughout my counseling, and I cried and I cried on my way out. I was surprised by my own reaction, but it told me that this was definitely the place for me to be at this moment in time. The healing starts here. (Note: But even in here, I could sense something weird, little signs and words spoken that made little sense to me and definitely did not belong in a counseling session. It made me anxious and invited distrust.)

It is challenging to meet all my suppressed emotions. I have been running from this my whole life. I have medicated myself with drugs, and I have spent most of my life in solitude and with running, because behind my friendly face were too many tears to count. But now that I know what it is about, I will do all I can to have my emotions flow freely, and I am trying to feel the outside from the inside again. I am feeling the outside from the inside again. It is okay for me to love my sexuality. It is okay for me to love my sexuality, and I find it completely natural to touch my skin and make it feel good, simply because it is natural with being a woman. And I am a natural woman. My belly is from my vagina to my chest, strong and reliable. Before I used to breathe in my belly, but now I breathe all the way down to my butt. My belly is tight and muscular and strong, and my lower back is very much supportive to my belly. My rib cage and my lungs are lovingly rising and lowering itself at the pace of my breathing. My breasts are firm and beautiful. They fit my shape and give me curves and femininity. I am proud of my upper back and my shoulders. In my spine, I hear the tingling voice of Jesus Christ, our Savior. My spine goes from my butt to my head. My neck is solid and strong, and my spine is electrifying and sending small vibes out through my body. I love my spine, and I love my back. My neck holds up my head. My hair is soft, and my eyes are peaceful. A nose, mouth, chin, and cheekbones are the essentials of my facial signature. My teeth are white and strong, and my tongue is wonderful and relaxed in my throat. I will now spend a minute or two just feeling this body and move back into my skin. My skin is soft as soft can be. This person is of good nature, and this person is me, Ruby Lee.

(Note: When I wrote this, I could not really feel my body. I was trying to create an inner image of my body and so connect my brain to the various parts of my body in order to take it back and to feel comfortable in it. Now, a year later, I am more together in my sense of being than I have ever been. My body is almost working again. I could even run the other day. What I focus on now is to feel the outside from the inside again. I focus on the inner energy body. Right underneath your skin is a field of energy. If you close your eyes and focus on this energy, you actually take away a lot of fear, and you increase your ability to heal. You are more than a physical body. You are also an energy body. Or your whole self is energy, really—pulsating and lively energy.)

Connecting Myself to My Emotions

I am sitting in the chapel. How do I feel about that? For the time being, I guess it is okay. I can now feel wholeness in my feet. I feel taller and actually all together as a person. No, not a person, a woman. And I am proud to say that I am a survivor and a woman. I just learned that expression here in the shelter. A survivor is slightly different than a troubled person with something wrong. I am a singer, and I try to rebuild my confidence on my blessing in my voice. I have been blessed with a good vocal range, and I cannot wait for the sunshine in my belly to be turned on. Yes, Lord Jesus Christ, I want it, and I want it bad. No one can steal my joy. And thank the Lord for earplugs. Yes, it helps. All the cackling women in here turn to "nerve-pills" friendly airwaves. My heart is beating, and my chest is moving to the beat of my breathing, and my hand is holding a pen. And the amazing movement of my wrist and fingers, arm and shoulder, all the way to my neck and brain makes it possible to write these letters, and my eyeballs measure the distance and interpret all the color vibrations that make distinctions in the picture I see. If that in itself is not amazing, then you try it and see. And my heart is still beating in my chest. If you snore, you breathe correctly, by the way. Deep breath, focus only on the out-breath. It is Sunday, and I did not go to church. That's just perfectly okay. I can go wherever I want to go. I am a free human being, and I feel what I feel when I feel it, and that's okay. I also react according to my emotions out from a wish-myself-well perspective. I like nice, clean, and rich surroundings. I like a little luxury and jewelry, and I love my sword and shield. And I am honored, Lord, that you have chosen me to be a carrier of your words. A picture of love; a heart that beats with a message to it, an edgy edge, and no doubts. My thoughts go to a lady who works here, Lord. She is in the intensive care unit. Please, Lord Jesus, make her well. Heal her. Have her wake up again and be strong. Will you, please! I really liked her. I send all my love over her, Lord, all over her hospital bed, revitalizing her heart. Help her start, Lord. Bring her back, please. I love you! Yours sincerely, Ruby Lee. And also, please help me heal emotionally and give me the wisdom to act upon my feelings. And I want to feel good—good, glad, glowing, and gorgeous. I wish to go where my heart finds joy: on a stage with lights, beats, fire, and balls. My belly navel is glowing. My belly navel is glowing. And I easily feel the outside from the inside again.

Afraid to Feel

I have been sexually abused and assaulted many times over many years. I thought it had to do with my own emotions, but I was so wrong because it had nothing to do with me. It had nothing to do with me at all—not my emotions, not my spirit, not my body, or my actions. It had all to do with the sickness of the devil, my mother, and a few more. But I would get reactions on my emotions, so I was not sure if all people could actually feel what I felt, and then I would be in danger, because then I would be assaulted. I grew terrified of my own emotions. My body is my body, and my spirit and I will rest in it forevermore here on planet earth. I am observing my own emotions from within, whatever on the outside I can handle or avoid. Emotions change all the time. They never stand still. It is energy. And my body is too. I am now going to see a movie, *JFK: Reckless Youth*, and for the first time, I'll focus on what this movie makes me feel.

And so I went to bed, didn't finish the movie. I felt tired. Must say it was good to sleep in the dorm again after being in a roach room. I toss and turn all night long and don't really feel very rested when I wake up. But it is a beautiful day, and the Lord woke me up in it. My body feels so much stronger, almost as a full organism. And it is time to feel the world from the inside again. So now I am doing my laundry and waiting for breakfast together with my friend. I'll go to the library today and watch M&M's interviews. I am somehow in denial. Double denial, if you could say that—both within myself and outside myself. I think I am in a hospital. It certainly feels like it. And I do believe someone is paying for something. I don't know what, though, so I will just focus on my breathing and healing and feeling. I guess the answers will reveal themselves after a while. And I feel the outside from the inside again. I have two appointments this week: one on Wednesday with the sexual assault center and one on Friday with my counselor at a room in the inn.

A child is like an emotional amoeba. You need to shape and form and teach them without taking away their emotions. They are honest, loving, and sincere unless you cover them with fear. And they are keepers of instinct. They can feel danger or intentions in other people. If you listen to their voices, then you allow them to put down their own boundaries. If you force them to go, even though they are scared, you break down their ability to make their own healthy boundaries. And later in life, they might find themselves in dangerous situations without recognizing it, because their parents told them not to listen to their own instincts. I posted a tweet, and right after, M&M posted one too. If he is the Birdman, then I am listening to him right this moment. I don't want to be numb anymore. I want to feel alive and breathing, energy flowing and heart beating. I have so many tears in my chest. They haunt me at night, and I can't find no rest. It is a test, terrifying and replying. The Birdman is my hope.

I need to give my testimony to tell people how God has worked in my life. And he sure has worked wonders, and He has been quite busy with me. This is the day when I will remember where I came from. Drug abuse, fear, constant stress, depression, sexual abuse, disconnection from my body, fear of all people. Living in darkness, being demon possessed and crying, mostly silent to the air, or maybe God has counted my tears and will replace them with joy at the right moment in time.

So I am starting to feel. And I should trust what I feel. I'd been a magnet toward bad people because they were the ones I was forced to be around when I grew up. When I now am able to recognize them, I can steer away from them because they are not fruitful for my spirit. I've heard enough crook stories. I don't really care about the stories. I've heard them before. Or I never could stand the crook stories, and I still can't stand them. So then I can walk away. Lord, I don't know what I know any longer. But I do know that I am feeling better, and for that, I am grateful. I know life doesn't give you happy feelings all the time, but I want them all. Because that is what living is about: living according to your own emotions and in correlation to your surroundings.

Save Your Soul

You can't conquer nature with science: scientific, political, and economic powers conquer one another and imprison us. And we all fall together that way. I don't understand what my surroundings are trying to teach me. When I get bored, it is okay to walk out of there. What do I really like to do during a day? I like to write, watch movies. I like to read. What you need to be preaching about / talking about is how to save your soul. Your own soul is what we are all fighting for. We are fighting for our own soul. Save my soul, achieved that goal.

I don't understand what is going on around me, Lord. And that worries me. I feel I'm being watched by someone whom I don't know. And I don't like it. I don't. I really need to get out of this situation, Lord. Please help me heal. I am begging you, please help me heal. Lord, please give me the wisdom and trust in my heart so that I will know what to do.

There is a truck running outside the store, and it made me nauseous to hear it, because it reminds me of my dead father. It creates a terror feeling in my chest. Stand in the emotion, feel it, and gradually, it will go away. I feel like running, but I cannot run anymore. I'll stay in my emotions. I breathe and feel. I think I am angry. I think it is anger flowing inside me. Today I have an appointment with a counselor at the sexual assault center. That's where the healing starts, I guess. I am at Amin's laundry room, and I feel like I am wasting my life away, but I guess I'm wrong. I think I'm starting my life today. It is a process. And the process is the beginning of my success because I will sing my songs. God gave them to me, and for that, I am forever grateful. It will be a full circle the day I perform again. I've practiced so hard. I've worked so hard. I've spent my whole life trying to improve my character and become a better person. When all this is done, I will look better than ever. I will be stronger than ever. I will feel better than ever. I will care more than ever. I will love more than ever. I will understand more than ever. I will be together with my matching man, one who can accept my strengths. I need someone who has been down the same road as I have. Together we shall form a musical style never before heard, with a message and a goal and strong enough to change the world. And I have learned so much from being here. I have a bed, I have a day, and I have the right to speak my mind. Be aware that a lot of people don't like that, especially those with secrets to hide. I have many strengths, and one of them is to expose evil. Jesus Christ, please help me cleanse my body from demons. Please help my eyes to see. Please help my ears to hear. Please help my heart to feel.

I wish for a record contract. And I wish for artist management. I wish for a paycheck to get me situated in a nice house with a garden to it; a house to live in, a house to love in; a living room with CDs and good sound speakers all around, a drawing/painting table, books, writing space, sofa, chair, table, TV and DVD, computer connection; a bedroom with a big bed, a walk-in closet with nice clothes, dim lights and green color, bed table and nightlight; a bathroom with bubble bath and shower; a music room—a magic music room with delightful softness and nice spaces for my instruments. I want an acoustic guitar, a Les Paul, a Vox amp, drums, a Fender Rhodes piano, harmonicas, bass, and a beat machine. Outside I want a porch with a swing and chairs on it, dreamcatchers, thread curtains, and light. In my music room, I would also need a microphone and a recording mic, a black one called "What Legends Are Made Of." And I would have a guestroom and a children's room and, in the house with me, a wonderful husband, the significant other sharing loyalty and respect, desire and passion and love. To be alone together, see if we could be that strong, living together side by side through ups and downs providing strength and support; A family at last.

And now I am at the beginning of my dreams, in Amin's laundry room, with my coffee and cardamom, in Nashville, Tennessee. Residing at a homeless shelter, a full circle—from a homeless home to a homeless shelter. There is a big difference between the two: security. And this is where I am, about to start making a difference in my life. And I start here by wiping away shame, guilt, and self-punishment in the forgiveness of our Lord Jesus Christ.

A CHANGE OF HEART

I want to change the world. And the only way to change the world is for me to change my ways and become more Jesus-like, become a better person. And I ask you to help me change the world. Because if you change a little bit and become a better person too, then we two have already changed the world. It takes one change at a time, and the responsibility lies within each and every person on this planet, Earth, that we all live on. I don't care if you are purple or blue, filthy rich or poor, a politician or a housecleaner. To me, a person is a person, period. If you can read what I write and talk to other people, then you are equal. You don't even have to be able to read or write to be equal. All people are equal. We all just do different things in our lives and, thereby, fulfill different purposes. And thank God for that. It would be mighty crowded in the Oval Office if everyone were to be a president. No, we are all born with our own purpose in life, and each and every one of us deserves to be happy. And happiness does not come from what society wants you to think. Society tells you that if you are a public persona with nice clothes and a heavy bank account, you should be happy. And if you are beautiful, you should be happy. And so the story goes. What really makes you happy is to meet a person who has changed himself a little bit to become a better person. It is when the intentions, the motives, and the ulterior motives come from a pure and honest place within a person that you actually change the world. Then you find support, trust, unconditional love, sharing, and acceptance of your character to fully understand that you are a good enough you as you. Everyone wants to be seen and taken seriously. I take you seriously, and I am grateful for every eye that reads these letters, because without a reader, there would be no author. So thank you for your time. If you truly want to change your life for the better, you need to sort out your thoughts and what you are thinking. People may not hear what you think, but the energy you send out is the same as if you spoke the words. So if you give a compliment to someone, make sure it comes from the heart. If you say "You look good in that color" and you think *Hah, she looks fat in that color,* you would do yourself a bigger favor if you did not speak at all. If you change your focus away from comparing yourself from that other person, you may actually be capable of seeing if she actually looks good in that color or not. The tiny sense of pleasure you get from comparing yourself really only lasts for a moment in time. The other person may not hear your thoughts, and the other people around may find you a nice person because of the compliment, but none of this really matters, you see, because God can hear your thoughts, and He is disgusted by such behavior. That is why a change of heart is so essential for your well-being. True beauty comes from the inside, and getting rid of the comparing, jealous behavior is a key to true beauty. The thing is, it needs to be sincere. It may not be the first time you say this, but with a little practice, it is amazing what you can train your brain to do.

THE BLAME GAME

It seems to be a trend to play the blame game. I do not wish to feel the way I feel, so I blame it on you. Today I woke up feeling down and out. I started to curse my surroundings but took myself by the scruff of my neck and said out loud, "I need to take responsibilities for my own emotions." I realized that the emotion actually lives within me, and there was no one around, so there could not have been any other source for my sadness than myself and my memory bank. It was the memories of my mother's betrayal. It is hardened energy in my chest, and as I stretch out the harshness, the emotions come back. And so I suddenly cry as a little girl, because the betrayal happened when I was a little girl, but I could not let out my sorrow at that point in time, so I contained it. I can now choose to go on and be mad at my mother who is not even here, or I can go on and take responsibility for my own emotions. I take responsibility for my own emotions by acknowledging the emotion and letting it be and just feeling it and letting it out. That way, I cleanse my system and free myself from the chains of sorrow. It is easy to blame someone else for your own emotions, but really, you are always in charge of your own emotions. The minute you start to blame someone else for your emotions, you actually give away your energy and your power. If I start to think about my mother and be angry with her, I send my energy to her and lose the focus within myself. If I choose to focus within myself and work on my emotion, I keep my energy, and I free myself from the memory. This is also a major part of forgiveness. If you choose to forgive, you cut off the energy pathway to your past. Forgiveness means letting go of the blame game and taking charge of the here and now. I breathe, therefore I am. I think, therefore I was. When you blame someone else, you give your power away, and then you are dependent on them to fix it. If you take responsibility for your own emotions and actions and outcomes, you yourself are the only one you depend on to fix it. You could say "He did this, and he needs to pay for it," or you could say "This happened, and here is what I feel about it, and I need to deal with that."

YOUR OWN ISSUES

In my life, I have had a lot of issues to work on. I knew that I had a lot of issues to work on. I also knew that I had to work on those issues in order to get through them. I took responsibility for the consequences of other people's behavior because in the end, what they did is not the big issue here. The big issue is how what they did affected me, and by knowing that, I can deal with the consequences of other people's behavior without giving away my energy to them. How I choose to deal with these consequences is on my own account. Because of my experiences, I know what it feels like to be miserable, which is why I choose not to make other people feel miserable. To live through these things, I focused on other people's well-being instead of my own misery. I used my knowledge to try and help them get along better with their lives and show them a way of thinking that made them smile more. Sometimes they would say "But you are not doing all these things yourself," upon which I would respond, "Just because I am not there yet doesn't mean that I can't share my knowledge with you. And you can choose to use it or not, but at least now you know." And it gave a purpose in my own misery to help other lost souls along the way, and I did change a lot of lives that way. I took my own issues and turned them into something positive. I knew my process would take the time it took anyway, so I chose to help other people along the way.

ADOPTING TWO CHILDREN
FOR A WHILE

When my ex and I had a fight once, his kids were there, and when they saw that I was going to leave, the girl said, "But you, Ruby Lee, you don't need anyone because you have *us*." And I knew that neither their mother nor their father cared for them, and so I said to the girl, I would be back and help them. I was really sick at this point in time, but I could not let her and her brother have no one to care for them. I had already given them clothes and things and their own room.

The little boy didn't talk at all when I met him, and I put a lot of energy into having him trust me. I would stand and smile at him from a distance so that every time he looked up, he saw a friendly smile. And that made him look up a little more often. He was afraid of his father.

And the girl said, "It is not my job to be teaching him everything." I said, "No, it's not your job. It's a grown-up job, really. I must say, though, now that you already got the job, you are very good at it!" What could I say? She was absolutely right.

Well, when I finally got out of the relationship, I remembered the girl's saying, and I just had to follow up on it. So I contacted the mother and asked if I could spend some time with the children, and she said yes. So I would pick them up after kindergarten and make dinner for them. Their room was a mess, and the mother was mostly dealing drugs in her kitchen.

I would ask her close to Christmas while she was making some gifts, "Oh, are you making a calendar for the kids?" I was highly positively surprised. And she said, "No. For the kids? I am making it for me!" And that just had my jaw drop to the floor.

"Well," I said, "I can make them a Christmas calendar then." And so I did. The mother reluctantly gave me some money for it, and the rest of the money I got from my sister. And I walked all around the stores to find them something nice. It is custom in Norway to have gift calendars for the kids in December. I found some nice things and wrapped up fifty gifts, nicely wrapped and the best things I could afford. And I delivered the gifts to the door. I did it so that they could have something to be proud of in their social life, something to bring and show off so they could stand out a little bit. I also carried all old things out of their room and up to the attic and put in some thread curtains and lights to make it nice in there.

I talked to the mother, and I was pissed off by her behavior, and I said aloud, "You don't care. You just simply don't care about them." And I knew I had crossed a line, so I walked into the girl and said, "I said something I should not have said, and I don't think you will see me for some time." I never said a negative word about their mother or their father. I was merely there for the children.

Before I left for Nashville, I went back to visit the mother, and she had learned her lesson, and she said "I have let my children down." And

I said, "What you say right now tells me that you haven't let them down. You have given them a mother, and children always love their mother. It is never too late to change and to become a mother in a good, loving way."

I know that they now have a home to live in, and I am glad I did it, even if it took a lot of my strength when I was down and out myself. In the aftermath, I say that it was absolutely worth the while. The little boy heard one of my recordings, and the second he heard my voice, he lit up with the biggest smile, got on his feet, and ran over to me and jumped into my lap and gave me the biggest hug.

GET THROUGH DRAMA TRAUMA

First of all, you must acknowledge what happened to you. For me, it was almost impossible to deal with the molestation, and still it is hard to admit that that is exactly what happened to me. But by admitting it, I also give way to a healing process. All the contained emotions linked to the wrongdoing in a trauma needs to come out. That is why I stress so badly that the role of a child's caretaker is also to hold them and to comfort them after traumas. You cannot overlook it because it makes you feel bad to talk about it. You have to be there for a child after things like this happen. Nobody really wants to have these experiences, but in my history, I know the importance of a comforting touch and being held by a mother. I learned it through lack of it. I know that a lot of my issues today would not have been there had my mother been there. A hug activates a whole lot of good reactions in your body, and it deactivates the bad energy that is being put into violent actions, whether they are emotional or physical. A loving, positive energy deactivates negative energy. Love has in it the power to conquer fear. There are no shortcuts in a healing process. If you talk to your doctor, he may put you on mood stabilizers, but this is not treatment! "Happy pills" are just containing your pain. You dull it down in order not to feel them. You do not work through them and make them disappear. There are no shortcuts in healing. Healing takes the time it takes. Just know within your heart that no person is born to be unhappy and down. There are certain things that make you this way. Pray for healing. Pray that the Lord can show you reasons for your problems or your roadblocks to happiness. He will reveal it to you through Jesus Christ, the Healer. What you are aware of, you can change. In my song "MizzUndaStood," I sing about these issues. I say, "What I am aware of I can change and take charge of my life again." Remember what you were like before the incident, and aim to get back there, to be a free version of yourself. The emotional, physical, spiritual, sexual, or whatever boundaries have been broken in you, you can repair them and become whole again. I believe that God is all-powerful, and being all-powerful, He is the Master Healer. Remember that doctors have been educated by people's knowledge of people. And mostly, doctors fix your physical troubles, but the emotional troubles show themselves in physical appearances to give you a clue of what may be wrong. Doctors can help you ease your pain or whatever, but they do not sell lasting solutions in a pill. Sometimes if things are worn out, you may need what the doctors prescribe for you, but the pill industry is a multibillion-dollar industry, and someone is making a lot of money on your behalf. I would look to the doctor for a relief but not for lasting solutions after traumas. If you are in an accident, it is different because doctors have the knowledge of the physical body, and thank God for that because they can perform miracles and fix you. But nowadays, people rush to the doctor merely to fix everyday problems like losing your joy or your soul. And they don't teach that in physical knowledge of the body. You as a person consist of more than a body. You have a physical you, a spiritual you, an emotional you, and a mental you. By making a conscious decision about your own well-being, realizing your own issues, and stopping the blame game, you have a good start on dealing with trauma drama.

YOU HURT MY FEELINGS

I learned from growing up being insulted and humiliated all the time in my home that it is smart not to attach yourself to everything that comes your way. I learned that it didn't really matter what was being said, it was more important how I took it. People get easily hurt by all sorts of things. Sometimes it is not even what is being said that really hurts. It may be wounds placed upon you years ago. It could be something that happened even in your childhood that you are not yet aware of. So in life, it may be that you need to go work on your own emotions instead of blaming "real time" for your reactions to "past time."

By comparing themselves to one another, girls get easily hurt by all sorts of things. Instead of being hurt by these things, they should honor the beauty from within, not the picture of beauty that society is trying to sell you through all sorts of products. True beauty lies in a happy soul.

LIFT PEOPLE UP

If you see a person who is down, don't feel happy because you feel better than them. Try and lift them up to your level of joy instead. You have to see people from where they are at, not from your own standing. You have to understand what their needs are, do not put your own standard upon them. When you talk to people, you use words. Whether you choose positive words or negative words, you will still use words. You may just as well choose uplifting words as down-talking words, because it feeds you in a better way, and the number of words you will utter is still the same, no matter which way you choose to put the words. (1) Positive talk lifts the spirit in front of you. (2) If the words align with your heart, you lift your own spirit. By doing this, you already made the world a little bit better by changing the energy in it. And you are one step closer to one of the fruits of the spirit, namely joy. The Bible stresses the commandment "Love thy neighbor as thyself." If you were down and out, how would you have liked for someone to treat you? The way you would have others be toward you, be so with them also. If something hurt you and you know how that feels, don't do that to someone else. If a certain thing uplifts you, then do this to other people. Why? (1) You learn from your mistakes and experiences, which mean that you are on the road to take your full potential as a person. (2) You give the fruits of your experience by not adding it to other people. I would say, "In nature, something gets born and takes on its full potential and then dies. Human beings, on the other hand, get born, do not take on their full potential whatsoever, and then die."

I received letters from my uncle in faraway Ethiopia when I was a child. He and his family were there to do missionary work. I remember those old film rolls and on it rolled pictures of starving children with no clothes and big bellies. I remember those hungry children, and I feel so sorry for them. I wrote poems about them, and I collected money from a yard sale to send to them. We got our picture in the paper, and the money was hopefully shipped off to someone in need. What it showed me at an early age was that there are people in worse situations than we complain about. And it was a way for me to aim my negative emotions and experiences into something positive, which is also my wish for this book. Do to others as you would have them do for you.

HOW ARE YOU TODAY?

"I'm fine. How are you?" is an empty politeness phrase. "Oh, on second thought, I haven't really thought about that. Is that important? Am I not just supposed to..." Hold your horses and get your ducks in order, which means, be quiet for a little while and recognize that there are four emotions to be aware of: (1) emotionally, (2) physically, (3) mentally, (4) spiritually. We are spiritual beings embodied with the ability to think and feel. We, as spiritual beings, feel things, and that makes us take action. We have our brain to make plans and find solutions with for our spiritual being to thrive. The body is your home, and it needs nourishment for the energy to flow freely. For example, today I feel relaxed. I went through my emotions, and my brain is quiet. I get some thoughts about this and that trying to intrude my peace and make me weary, but I just let them pass by without feeling or reacting upon them. Physically I feel so much better than I did six years ago. Each and every punch or beating leaves a mark and a tension. When you release these tensions, they go away, and you can relax again. For example, if a child falls and hurts itself, you would pick up the child, and with love and care, you would have your fingers gently stroke over the wound and comfort the child. One, you release the physical damage, and you soothe the emotions and the fear that follows an injury. That way, you as a mother/father will erase the harshness of the energy that is being put into an injury. Emotionally I feel relaxed, and my emotions are not overly excited or overly down. So I feel maybe a little excited but relaxed. Spiritually I feel connected. I pray and talk to God in my head / mentally. To be present and aware in the moment is to be aware of all your emotions and be true to them. If you feel relaxed mentally, relaxed physically, relaxed emotionally, and relaxed spiritually, then your answer would be a truthful *"I feel good!"* If you are unaware of your four emotional states, it will have you confused as a person. Seek you first the kingdom of God, and the rest shall be added unto you. The kingdom of God is pureness and love and caring. When you wish for happiness—true happiness, that is, not the one you buy in a gadget of some sort, but the one that is lasting—you have to work on your spiritual well-being as well as the other more apparent states.

MY BIRTHDAY AND
NEW CHALLENGES

Today is my birthday, June 7, my "new birthday" at thirty-five years of age. I feel better than I have since my day of birth. My story has been a tale of trials and tribulations. I have spent numerous hours putting myself together from being torn into bits and pieces into becoming who I am today. And today I feel somewhat whole again. I still have some healing work left in my body, and I still have to share my story in order to close this first chapter of my life. I tell my tale not to gain sympathy and have people feel sorry for me but in order to share with you the knowledge and wisdom God has put on my heart through experiences and a deep longing for joy and also what is possible with God. The past is already passed, and yet I have all the good things left of life to learn. I did not speak in *I* form until I was twenty-nine years of age. Someone told me "You need to start talking for yourself" because I would say "If one did this or that, could this or that then be the result?" And so it was very hard for me to use the *I* form. And still if you ask me who I am, I would say "I am," and not really know what to add to "I am." I am not familiar with acting on my emotions, and so I have a whole area of my life yet to discover. I must find my likes and dislikes and my dos and don'ts. And I can tell you that I wish to share my knowledge with anyone who wishes to hear it, but I don't really know what it is that people might want to hear. Or what they might need to hear. I think they already know everything I know and more, or I don't understand them. And I get stressed out sometimes because I think that everybody knows all that I know and more. And so I feel I come in short and often fall out of relations due to that. I am trying hard to change all these things, and I wish to release my music and my story. I wish to have a band and make music. I wish to walk next to someone special. I really long for a hand to hold and someone to sleep next to and to feel the warmth of another person, sharing my thoughts and views with him. Having someone to share my days with and hold and touch and hug. I just have no idea of how to get there. In my imagination, I often think about M&M because I really do relate with a lot of his words. And I know people might see him as a disruption, but I see a softer side in him when I hear him speak and in his songs. I think he would match me really well. We could make revolutionary music together and have fun. I need to work on my identity, I guess. I like to learn things, make music, and write and sing and make people happy. In Nashville, a lot of things go on around my head, but to be honest, I don't really understand it and, even less, what to do about it. And I do wish to share my knowledge with all people who wish to hear, but I don't know how to go about that either, and so I write this book in order to have things happen, hopefully, in my life. I am not used to such quiet days, and I like to have things to do. I need some action, and my present situation is not satisfying those needs, though I am very blessed to have friends who take me into their homes and are friendly toward me in this new situation in my life. They are helping me in all possible ways to be grounded and present and ready to focus on my future. And I am soul-searching because all I really wish for is to be happy.

GOD IS ALIVE AND WELL

"Lord, I thank you for my second chance. Lord, I thank you for this second dance. And I'm praising your holy name / out of darkness, into holy light. No more crying, I am smiling bright, and you guided me all the way / I was broken, I was close to dead, but your healing, it woke me up instead, now I'm singing a song of praise / and I thank, Lord, I thank you. I thank you!"

I can proudly say that I wrote this song just the other day. Things are not that bad if I can make a song from it, I used to say as a child. And I still claim the same thing. Making songs makes my whole life worth living. I hope you get to hear them someday. My songs are from all and everywhere in a lifetime of searching and finding the grace of God.

FINDING GOD

If there is one thing I wish I had done sooner in my life, it would be to read the Bible and listen to the Word of the Lord. Because the recipe for good living was already written two thousand years ago, so why are we complaining really? Just saying...When I came to Nashville and the Church of Christ, I came to realize one thing of massive importance: God has been guiding me through this process ever since I was a child. How would I know that? Well, many things are telling me that the good Lord has a purpose for my living. I would not be here today if I had not been touched by his holy light. Here are some incidents from my life that I believe could not have happened if it was not by God's hand.

THE DREAM AND STANDING
UP FOR MYSELF IN COURT

Take the dream for instance. After the dream with the arrows, I did not dream about this till years and years later. When I dreamed it again, I heard the voice calling, and I turned around, and my earthly father stood up on a hill and looked at me. I turned around and met his eyes. An eye for an eye, good meets evil. When I was in Nashville, at the rescue mission, my father came to take me away. I panicked completely at that moment, and the police, thank you very much, took me down to the police station, and I pressed charges against him. When I received the letter from the court, I almost went into a comatose state of mind. I wanted to drop out of it, but on the note, it said my name versus my father's name. For this reason, I could not do other than to face the truth and face my rights as a person. Strangely, I felt like the criminal. In the courtroom, he claimed my name, but I said, "Madam, that is my name." It may be hard to understand the importance of this for someone from outside a family system like ours. I can just say that he knew what he was doing. I took the stand and told the judge that this man had physically, mentally, emotionally, and sexually abused me for fifteen years. It took me a little more than fifteen years to cut all contact with this devilish manifestation of a person. He passed last year, bless his soul. I forgive him and let it all go. Only the Lord can be a judge over our actions here on planet Earth. But I did get a stay-away order from the judge, and this is the first time my side of the story has been taken into consideration. I finally felt that someone believed me and protected me. The Land of the Free—God bless America.

A LONG ROAD TO FIND LOVE

S urrounded by evil and with a lack of love in my upbringing I was
taught one thing; everyone deserves to be loved. They treated me
so badly in my home that I turned toward the opposite; I would treat
everybody very nicely. My memory of all the abuse was taken away
from me for many years. For twenty years, I could not understand
why I was acting the way I was. I asked why. But I asked it due to
my own behavior. I did not understand my own self. Now in the
aftermath, I can see that I was in shock and terror all the time. Like
my doctor said some years ago when I said I was freaking out again,
"I don't think you are freaking out. I think you are terrified." And it
was not until he told me that I knew he was right. I was terrified, and
I didn't know it because I was so used to being afraid that it no longer
came to me as anything unusual. Not until he told me—then I could
finally deal with my frightened inner being. I did not relax until I was
around thirty years of age. I thought I had felt relaxed before this
also, but what you don't know, you don't know till you know it, and
that can be a variety of things. I didn't know how it felt like to relax
until I relaxed for the first time, and then I said, "Oh my goodness,
what a difference!" During these twenty years, I learned a lot about

human behavior because I was looking for the real smile, the one that starts in the belly and naturally comes out in your face.

I wrote a song: "My ambition in life is to smile. To ride the victory ship and raise the flag in the end, even though I've cried. It's not meant to be easy, but I'll try." And, boy, am I glad I did. I am smiling from every cell in my body at this moment in time, listening to the song He put in my heart. I spent twelve years asking people questions about why they did what they did, and it took me seventeen years to find out that I had been communistically brainwashed. Now I have spent six years on physical healing. My arms were so twisted that you could see it just by looking at them. My spine had been twisted. My neck had a crack in it. I could not feel my neck. I only knew it was somewhere in between my thoughts and my toes. I could not feel my own physical appearance. Now I can feel the wind on my skin. My body was in a total muscle defense, and I asked a "breathing therapist" if he could see where I had been beaten, and he looked over my whole body and just shook his head. I later asked him if he thought I could ever be free from this muscle defense. He said, "No, because you have to go to the outer limits of what a person can take." I think that was back in 2008, and ever since that, I have gone to my outer limits on each and every muscle in my body. Year after year, I spent ten to twelve hours a day easing up old tensions. First, find the muscle. Second, focus your attention on it. Third, put all your energy into that moment and hold. Gradually the muscle tensions will let go. I asked my doctor in Norway, after spending two years on my legs. When I thought I was done, I found that it was much worse on the other side, and this went on and on and on, back and forth. So I ran to my doctor and asked, "Are we people layers and layers of muscles or something?" And he said, "Yes!" I wanted to cry at that point because I knew I had a whole lot of work ahead of me. What can I say? God is the Healer! It may take awhile, and you have to be willing to receive it. And *believe* in it. I wrote in a song, "How many tears can you cry before you dehydrate? Endless, if you believe."

TALKING TO GOD

I think God sees what you do toward other people. "Love thy neighbor as thyself," he says, and I think kindness and a loving heart will take you far in this world. I started to pray in Oslo, though I talked to God long before this moment in time. I would actively pray the Lord's Prayer over and over and over again. I knew that in me were demons, not only from my own sins but also from my mother's betrayal in the attic. I felt and saw something darker than the dark coming into my right side, and after that, I could hardly hear what people said anymore. I could see them talking, but the words would not reach my brain. It was like wearing a cotton ball around my head. I sat by myself, isolated and alone. But after all the terror, I was glad to be by myself whenever I could. Stone caves, snow caves, and underwater snorkeling sum up my childhood vacation activities. Inside me was an everlasting movement of nervousness. In Nashville rescue mission, I prayed all the time and from one day to another. My whole behavior changed, and I knew that a demon had finally left my body, because stress doesn't just disappear all of a sudden and change your whole behavior from one day to another. In Norway, I also got some demons out of my body while I prayed the Lord's Prayer. How do I know this? I could feel the relief. Only God knows the real deal, but He showed me a bit of this truth from a human perspective. You may believe it or not, but I know that there is an ongoing war between good and evil, and it is a fight for your soul. I can assure you that you would want to be on God's side in this battle because human life only lasts a breath in the total measure of time. Your soul, however, lasts forever. The Bible says there is a burning lake of fire, worse than any human minds can really comprehend. I have tasted a tiny piece of hell on earth, and I sure as hell am not going to spend eternity down under. I can't underline the importance of baptism and a change of heart and a new way of living on planet Earth. I just know from my experiences that there is a true spiritual war, an ongoing and never-resting warfare between good and evil right here and right now. Do you want true joy? Do you want true love? Do you want a peaceful mind? Do you want true beauty? It is all from above and within; they are the fruits of the spirit. It is what God promises you if you live according to his teaching. And from experiencing both sides of the fence, I would say the choice is easy. I want to be on God's team. I choose happiness.

SENT BACK FROM DEATH

Another example of God's existence in my life happened when He saved me from death. Here is what happened. During my self-medicating period of drug abuse, I also had a near-death experience I think is worth mentioning. It clearly shows that God All-Powerful is alive and well—you better believe it, because He is real. I had been out a night drinking. It was shortly after my boyfriend died. I was twenty-seven years of age, and all my sorrow I kept inside. I met with some people and asked them for amphetamine. I had used that before but quit for two years when I moved to Oslo. They said they did. But when we got there, they had something else, something I was unfamiliar with. I just said I wanted it. It was GHB and is used to drug horses or something. I don't know, but I took eight tops of this, and normally you take 0.5 to one top, no more. So I quickly fell asleep, and the next I remember is that I was in a white room. It was very clean and tidy and bright. On my left side, I saw a shiny bright light. And I thought to myself that it was extremely nice and tidy there. After that, I remember creaking on the floor, and I thought that I was in a ghost house in the country. I saw only shadows of people sometimes, and I could not recognize their faces. I screamed "Help!" so hard that I had no voice left when I finally woke up. It was like being caught up in my worst nightmare, and I faded out again and woke up again several times. I woke up raped and naked, and I could not move my arms, so I had to ask a gay person in there to put my clothes on. He did, and I slowly got out of the bed. The room was a mess with clothes everywhere and just a tiny window with a streetlight on the left side of the bed. I went to the bathroom and vomited for a long time and got back into the living room, looking for my scarf. I reached my hand outside the couch, and I touched a snake. Yes, there was a snake in the room. I could only whisper; my voice was gone. They said I had not paid for the drug I got, and so I said I would. We went out to a 7-eleven store, and I gave her the money and bought myself a hotdog and also one for a homeless guy because he looked so hungry. I got back into my home and realized that it was Monday evening. I went out on a Friday. When I got home, I was awake for two days in shock. I read about this drug online and realized that I had been dead for a little while. I did not press charges or do anything about it. After all, it was entirely my own fault. I chose not to play "the blame game." All I can say is that if God did not have a plan for this life, I would not have been here today. So thank you, Lord! By the grace of God am I here today.

BALL SPORTS AND MUSIC

With the ball sport handball, I was quite successful. I managed the sport well and scored many goals and was a feared defense player. It gave moments of joy, sorely needed in darkened times of sorrow. My earthly father once had said to my brother that he was impressed by what I managed to do in this sport. I can understand his attitude now that I remember all the damage he did to me at such an early age. Again, with the damage, I could not have managed to do this but by the grace of God. After many years of success, I realized that it did not really bring me true joy. I just felt a little happy for a moment in time. And when the moment was gone, so was my joy. Therefore, I gradually gave up the sport and gradually fell deeper into drug abuse. I became an everyday user, medicating my emotions away from my conscious mind, and playing my part as the caregiver and always-smiling person. I wrote songs and dreamed about getting away from my mother and my birthplace. A drummer who played on my song in studio told me about a school in Oslo where you did not need all theoretical knowledge to be accepted. So I sent an application and started school there. I had several bands: Blue 24/7, Ruby Lee and Her Bees, and

BBBand...I got my song "Life Is Strange" played on the radio. So at least in this area in my life, things were bright and positive. But after came several incidents—my sweet boyfriend of two years died, and I was nearly killed at my job, got in a violent relationship, started to remember my early childhood abuse, dropped out of teaching school, quit my job, didn't finish music school, and quit my band. When my breakdown came, it was a blessing in disguise—I had to deal with the traumas in my life. I had to go through all my suppressed emotions. In 2008, I had a breakdown. I withdrew from everything and everywhere, I quit everything, and I focused only on my aching body. I was on penicillin for a year because my immune system collapsed. I was bedridden and in pain. Slowly I built myself back up. I got hold of a new apartment, and I got my instruments and my recorder. I got myself a bed, and underneath it was my studio. I recovered and recorded. And in 2012, I finally recorded my first album "...butAlive!!!" I play all instruments, and there are eleven songs awaiting release.

DREAM; TAKE OFF NASHVILLE

F ive years after my breakdown, I wrote a note. It said "Dream. Take off Nashville 12th of April 2013." I had already sent a copy to Third Man Records in Nashville, and I asked Jack White to produce it. He was the ambassador for the record store day, and so I had to be there by April 20 because I figured, if he was the ambassador of the record store day, he would be there. This was in March 2013. I had no idea where I would get $1,000 and more to buy a ticket and stay in Nashville three weeks. My "sick money" had been cut to the bone by unfaithful government workers, so I had no idea where to get money from. I went out and sat in a neighborhood apartment and talked about me going to Nashville. A homeless guy who had just sold his apartment came to this place, and he was bragging about having so much money that he didn't know what to do about it. So I said, "If you have all that money, maybe you can lend me some, because I really need to go to Nashville twelfth of April. It is my dream."

"How much does it cost?" he asked.

I said, "Maybe one thousand dollars."

And he pulled out $1,000—or 6,000 KR to be exact—from his pocket and said, "If this is all it costs to fulfill your dream, I will give it to you."

So two hours after I wrote the note in my apartment, I had the money to go in my hand. I put the money in my account and bought a ticket. He gave some more money to live on. I panicked the weeks before departing and gave my keys away to a homeless guy without a place to stay and jumped into a cab and never looked back.

I found myself homeless in Nashville, crash-landing into a new beginning. First, I had to get clean after ten years. I didn't think of that. I had no money—where would I live? I didn't think of that. My English was nearly gone from being absent for ten years. I didn't think of that. I didn't really have to think about it because God knew. He sent me to a place where there are churches everywhere. I have never been to a place with such strong love for God. As a homeless person in Nashville, you get the Word of God whether you like it or not, and I liked It. It was a place of comfort and peace, a place of hopes and dreams, a place of kindness and teaching, a place to be reborn again.

ONE YEAR DRUG FREE

I can proudly say that today I am one year drug free. I have little symptoms of my PTSD; I learned to live with it. My panic attacks are no longer present. My mind is sound and peaceful. My body is close to healed. I have read through the Bible. I have my own room to live in. I have recorded eight songs, written a lot of poems, and I have learned about how to live. I have forgiven my mother, my father, my brother, and my sister. I carry no blame for their wrongdoings. I take full responsibility for my own life. I have God. I have hope. I have a new beginning in my life, and I have yet to learn all the good things in life. All the good things about sharing.

And Jesus Christ did not die without reason. He died for sinners like myself so that I could be forgiven in His name and be made new in the Word of God. He gave me this story to tell because it is a living example of what the good Lord is capable of doing. He sent His only Son to die for our sins. The cross is your gateway to heaven but also your gateway to a happy life here on planet Earth. "You choose to be happy or not to be; it's your responsibility. You choose to be happy or not to be; it's a lifelong responsibility." So many choices—I go for happiness. And the Lord Almighty is alive and well!

POEMS AND SHORT WRITINGS
DURING THE SHELTER

I am not really a novel author. I am fond of writing poetry and short writings in time. When I came to Nashville, I would say it was a crash landing, and I was terrified! I had left behind everything I owned, and all I brought across the sea were two suitcases with unsuitable clothes. I was only going to stay here for three weeks, but my condition kept me from going back there. I had no money, so I lived on the street for a while. My friend in the wheelchair was looking over me when I slept, and he tried to teach me a thing or two. It was hard for me to be there, though; I was in panic. I do suffer from PTSD and panic attacks, and in addition to this, I also quit drugs cold turkey. And to be honest with you, I had not been without drugs or alcohol for more than one month at the longest since I was twelve years of age. After a little while on the benches downtown, I finally heard of the shelter, and on a Friday night, I took my two suitcases and my guitar and walked all the way up to the homeless shelter. Here I tried to cope and quiet my mind, getting into the routines of the shelter. I had the hardest period of my life in there, in one way, that is. I mean you do not choose to be beaten or misused or mistreated as a child, but you do choose to get free from the chains that have been put upon you. It has taken me over a year to clear my mind and work on my muscle defense. I have prayed every day and spent most of my time in the church. It is quiet there, and God is close. I needed to be in a place like that in order to manage to cope with my stress, and the people in the church having been amazingly good to me has made it a success story. While I was still in the shelter, I found myself with new dilemmas, and I had not planned to be here. I just knew I could not go back, because I would die if I did. And so I wish to share with you some of the poems I wrote and some of the nightly devotions and some of my short writings from that time.

POEMS AND SHORT WRITINGS
IN TIME FROM THE SHELTER

Homeless Dream

Sleeping women
Snoring women
Longing women
Scoring women
Homeless
Bunk-bed heaven
Praying
The man in my heart
Live together
Make art
Fart
For fun
Run
Catch me, kiss me
When?
Will my love
Take me home

I Am Grateful, Lord

I crash-landed in a distant town
Love is what I found
Behind me lay disappointments and darkness
Ahead of me,
Light, worship, and ashes

I am grateful, Lord
For I am breathing
I am grateful, Lord
For I am sleeping
I am grateful, Lord
For you have me seeing
That it is really very easy to be a
Human being

Observing Myself

Observing myself
from a new point of view.
There is a time for the old
and a time for
the new.
I have a clue of what to do.
I just don't grab it all
completely,
Yet,
But that would be my next step.
I put one foot ahead of the other,
one thing at a time.
I'm in the right place to start to do
What needs to be done.
Observing myself
from a new point
of view.

I Believe in Tomorrow

I believe in tomorrow
'cause yesterday is already gone.
I believe in tomorrow.
So I'll write another song.
I believe in tomorrow
So I leave behind old sorrow
I believe in tomorrow
'cause someone's love
enlightens my heart
Not much longer
shall we be apart
It's a melody
from heart to heart
Touches of hope
The best dope
"The hope of today,"
The Lord says,
"Shall be your days of tomorrow"

I believe in love
'cause my heart tells me
It is present.
I believe in love.
The future looks brighter than the desert.

I believe in love
'cause love has in it the power
to conquer fear
I believe in love
And I believe in you,
My dear.

A Modern Slave

A new slave
Slave to materialism
Slave to name-dropping
Slave to money-popping
Slave to image and surname discussions
Slave to this hierarchy so-called society
Slaves of industrialized silence
Slaved to invisible walls
Slaved to invisible fences
Slaved to mind capturing preinstallations
Dividing mind, body, and soul apart
Independence comes from the heart
A solid heart can play smart
And light up
The darkness

A Tradition to Be "Sheeple," People?

It's tradition to be sheeple instead of people.
Trends are changing, sheeple.
It's time to become people, people!

You have a mind of your own.
Walking in patterns already sown
Well known
By the enemy of this state
This smiling state
Are you happy?

Happy Wishes, Sheeple

Happy wishes, sheeple
Oh, independent people
Dreams do come true
They appear in blue
Blue as the whitening
Bright
Lightning
Let it rain
Love
Lord
'Cause love is all that is worth living for
Without it
There is nothing
And nothing takes a long time
When you live it
Give it
To yourself
And the rest will follow
'Cause in the end
My friend
Everybody is looking for
Happiness
Bless
Your neighbor
Without his knowledge
And love shall rain upon thee
In return
For it is all that the Lord is asking for
Your love
And kindness
And when you suffer along your route
The only remedy-boot
There is
Is love

And it's free
For you and me
It starts
In the hearts
Of each and every one of us
Which makes you special
And you are special
His special creation
Within this nation
Of dreams
It was built
Torn down by guilt
Guilty ego-chasers
Riding in correctness blazers
In through our TV screen
Made specifically for you to see
Special made for you and me?
Not really
Money makers
Happiness fakers
'Cause there is no love is commercial stuff
It's a money bluff
Puff, puff, and huff
Brick walled
Wallets
Pets
Petted by the people chosen
Reality arose'n
Politicians
Promises, promises turn to dust
In this game
Select a name
A made believe illusionist
Public deceive
Created for you and me
To see

To believe in the words of hope
Election dope
Predestined
Disillusioned fake hope
Vote dope
Hangman jury
Enrolled in jewelry
And pretty pictures
Painted by their color mixers
Enrolled in a world of their own
Numbers rarely shown
But they look right on the screen
Divided and decided
Deceive
Receive
This message of hope
Cut the dope
Hang on to a love rope
'Cause all you need is love
They said it in the sixties
And I guess
The sixties goes
Into all tomorrows
Take my advice
Be wise
Be good
And all your dreams
Shall be fulfilled by Him
Our love within
Ourselves
Is all that matters
And this specific matter
Is easy
You see
You own it
And it's for free!

By the Grace of God

By the grace of God am I here today
Gradually I learn to obey
I read his words in the Holy Book
It took
Awhile for me to see
That He's been calling out for me
Be
More,
He says
Yes
I say
I'm learning to obey
And by the grace of God am I here today
Obey your thirst, which is me,
He says,
I am your source
Of energy-giving pleasure!

Devotions

So how do you cope with not knowing what tomorrow
brings and with absolutely no plan in your mind and no
way to make a plan, when your surroundings cut you
short as a human being? Well, what I did was to write
my daily and nightly devotions. It puts your mind on the
important things that you actually can focus on while
everything around you is darkness. I wish I knew that in
the darkest hours in my room as a child, because I would
have felt security and also put my concentration on
what I could focus on in all and seemingly never-ending
darkness. So I learned to write those in the shelter, and
I will share some of them with you. Hopefully, you can
learn it too and actually enhance the sense of quality in
your life.

Just 4 Today

Just for today
I sit up straight.
Just for today
I am thankful for my life.
Just for today
I stay in focus.
Just for today
I surrender all.
Just for today
I do everything with love.
Thank you for guiding me
Lord Jesus Christ.

Just 4 Today, Marshall

It's another day, and I walk into it with love.
She said eight machines, and eight is the magic
marshmallow number.
I take that to be a good sign.
Just for today, I am going to stay focused
Because I need to be focused
To get out of here
I am going to sing my way out
And in order to do that
I MUST STAY FOCUSED.
Just for today
I do all things with love
I sit with love
I write with love
I talk with love
I walk with love
I wash clothes with love
I smoke with love

I dream with love
And I hope with love
I am cleaning out my closet
Doing my inner and outer laundry
Thank you
Emmmm Marshall.

Just 4 Tonight 1

Just for tonight, I am thankful for today.
I let go of today and write in the moment with love.
I surrender all and embrace my peace
I lie down with love
And I welcome the dreams of the night
My mind is sound
And I sleep with love
My body falls into place
And I heal in the night
I wake up happy, and I embrace a new day
A new day to get closer to my goal
Closer to my man
My perfect spouse,
M&M
Bless him, Lord Jesus Christ
Tell him I love him
Thank you

Just 4 Tonight 2

Just for tonight, I feel totally and fully peaceful.
Just for tonight, I close my eyes and welcome
The good darkness
The absence of light delights
My nerves

My muscles
And my thinking
My body bathes in comfort
And
When I wake up in the morning
I am fully rested
And glad for another day
Good night
Thank you, Lord Jesus Christ
I love you
I lie in my bed with love
I love myself
And I love dreaming, resting, longing
Awakening awareness
of my holy temple
My body

A Nightly Devotion

Just for tonight, I shall peacefully rest my eyes.
My mind is sound, and my sleep is deep.
I dream what I dream
And
when I open my eyes
tomorrow morning
I am ready for a new day.
I do all things with love
All things with love.

A Moment in Time 1

I can't sleep at night
And when I finally do
It's time to do a nothing or two.

Listen to a load of crap.
Who put me into this trap?
I am guessing all along
confused in my own song.
Everybody knows something I don't.
It's a game
A shame
Pulling me around like a puppet fool.
Left out of the knowing is all but cool
All I say seems to be known by all
Phones everywhere
Who am I to call?
I surrender all and call on Jesus
While putting together my bits and pieces
So while the world turns with its hidden expectations
I try and hold myself together
to be a person.

A Moment in Time 2

It's another day
And I already prayed for physical healing
A slow but efficient dealing
A living testimony and a light in the dark
the gift and the curse
of a loving heart.
So many people enwrapped in fear
Frightened to the point where they hardly dare
To put one foot ahead of the other
A lost generation is longing for a mother
A hardened heart is divided and apart
From everything that blooms
Widows and grooms
Reaching out for a spark of light
Searching outside for something within

A treasure sound asleep
In the deep
of every living person's inside.
The actions you make either give, or they take
From your always, forever, and present
Absence of fake
The Holy Book is a guideline
To what everybody is trying to find
and search for all life
long
Namely their own joy and happiness
song.

A Moment in Time 3

Today was a good day
My mood was shifting but stable the whole day
I ate breakfast with my friend
Coffee and bread outside the gas station again
Then evil came dropping by when my friend said
good-bye
"Escape," said the car
"Get far away from that woman"
And so I did
I went to my drug-addiction program
Triggers and self-esteem on the agenda
The weather has been all right all day
Fairly warm December day
Confidence
I am confident
And proud of who I have become
After the program, I stopped by the little church
Bible study and the Word of God
I like to listen to His Word
I wish the world was more like that.

Church was over at 3:00 p.m.
Back into the mission again
Night bag and clean clothes;
same bed, new bedroll.
Make my bed and lay my head
On a vibrating neck pillow
Sending chills and thrills through my bones.
Muscle contraction
Healing in action
Dinnertime after a shower
Dry turkey
And an hour
Before closed doors
Go for a walk
Focus on toes, heel, and ankles and roll
Smoke another cigarette and look at the moon
My mission here is over pretty soon
After roll call and praise reports
Draw a few pictures
Now I write
Before I close my eyes
I will read a little more
So tired

A Moment in Time 5

Flying cars or grounded stars?
Airwave of information
One true person to shake the nation
Airway information meets digitalization
Cars and people flying in the air
Conversations out in the atmosphere
Being a family person is different than the airline
version
Dreams, hopes, and aspirations

People blinded by college degrees and formal education
Preprogrammed and ready to receive
The deceive
And the closing of the heart
Play your part
And keep it open
I have dedicated the past six years to healing
And it is revealing
A sudden truth to me
Plastic people with money drive
Needs approval just to thrive
A code
Persona code
And a designer rode
Down the fashion alley
Far away from the happiness valley
Only to find something new
Something blue
A breath in time
No lasting dime

A Moment in Time 4

A glare of hope
Untangled from the strangling rope
I relax, I feel good
I'd do a million things if I could
I am going to try and remember who I am and how I feel
It's the two ingredients life requires to be real
Real, seal the future is my wish
I feel love in my heart
Heaven shoots dart
At me
Pulling me out of a dark that nearly consumed me
Perfumed me

Ruby Lee Tuesday

With tiny touches of a smell of hope
Because when all is a mess
Full of stress
From the morning till night
Every day, a flooding fight
Barely holding my head above water
I've been swimming in dirt on planet Earth
Earth shakes and milkshakes
Full force, confusion and no brakes
It takes
Determination and focus
To become whole when all has been broken down
Bones, muscles, spirit, and soul
What is my goal?
Because I am eligible for my own dream
I'm not dead
Not yet
In between, I have time to kill
And I wish to make it a flying thrill
Not alone but along with him
To M&M, my heart sings
We are the same in many ways
We've been the same places of hurt and disgrace
"Just lose it," he says
And I will do that
I am at a good beginning
Two more days
Weekends pass without my knowledge
Lord, I need a helping hand
On my next step
Because I haven't really thought of that yet
So I focus on my healing
My heart finally feeling
Love again
And, Lord,
I need a eureka idea
That sums up my life so far

BE AWARE OF WHAT
YOU WISH FOR

A nd be aware of what you wish for; your thoughts, they may come true, you know. I asked for a way to put together bits and pieces and make some sense out of my story. And here you have it. It is a mixture of poems, longings, bad memories, good memories, victory, and hope. Most of all, I hope that this story gives you hope. And I hope that you will consider reading the Bible and learn from history. I want to change the world, and the only way anyone can change the world is to have a change of heart. I challenge you to change yours. Be to others as you will have them be with you. And love God foremost of all. Because if you do, you will not love the means of the world more than you love the quality of life. I do not wish to die and not tell it, because it is so full of hope. Because if I can do it, so can you! I do not want anyone to feel sorry for me. That has never been my agenda. What has been *has been*, which means it is gone. It only remains in your memory. You can choose to bring it out this moment in time, but then you would have to live with it forever. And if you have been through hell once in your life, there really is no good reason for going there twice.

CHAPTER 2, FOR THE REST FOR THE BEST

I holler, Soul Man. Can you hear me? I actually can relate to your story. Dinner at 8:00 p.m.?

CONTACT INFORMATION

If you wish to contact me, you can do so on this e-mail address:
Loverebel68@gmail.com

My web page:
www.ladyloverebel.com

With all my love, I wish you all the best for the rest!
Better believe; it is worth it!
In God I trust, and He is alive and well.
Without Him, I could not have done anything.
Thank you, Lord!
I love you!